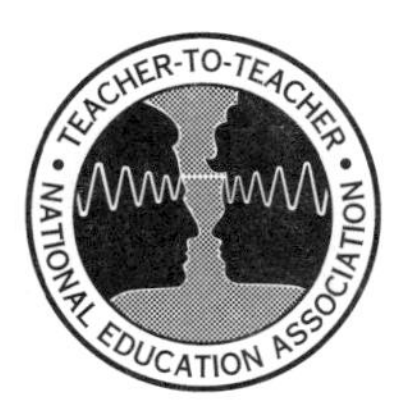

BEYOND TEXTBOOKS

hands-on learning

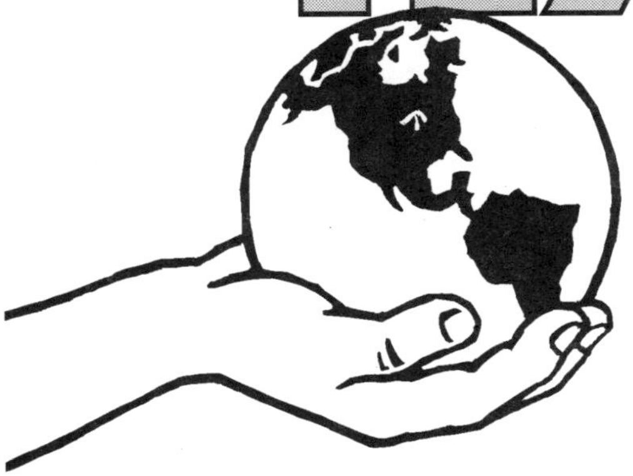

NEA Teacher-to-Teacher Books

Library of Congress Cataloging-in-Publication Data
Beyond Textbooks: hands-on learning.

Contents

How to Use this Book

Beyond Textbooks: Hands-On Learning is no ordinary book. It is one of a series from NEA Teacher-to-Teacher Books, in which classroom teachers speak directly to other teachers—like you—about their school restructuring efforts.

Printed in the upper right-hand corner of every book cover in the series, is a routing slip that encourages you to pass the book on to colleagues once you have read it—in other words, to spread the word about school change.

Book topics cover areas such as large-scale school change, student assessment, multi-age grouping, and inclusion.

Read the Six Stories

Inside each book you will find stories from six or more teachers across the country who discuss, step by step, how they tackled a specific restructuring challenge. They describe what worked and didn't work, and provide you with diagrams, checklists, or tables they think other teachers would find useful.

Write Your Own Ideas in This Book

At the end of each story in this book is an area called Reader Reflections. This area is for you and any colleague who reads the story to write related insights and action points for your school or school district to consider.

You see, the purpose of NEA Teacher-to-Teacher Books is not only to spread the word about school change, but to encourage other teachers to participate in its exploration.

Discuss Your Thoughts With Others

Once you have routed a book through your school, you can meet with colleagues who contributed to the Reader Reflections sections and expand upon your thoughts.

Go Online

Believe it or not, the communication and sharing does not have to stop there. You can discuss a Teacher-to-Teacher book series topic with teachers across the country. Any NEA member who subscribes to the America Online electronic network can participate in an ongoing forum on these book topics.

The National Education Association's area on the network is called NEA Online. Once signed on to NEA Online, just keyword to: *NEA Prof Library.*

To subscribe to NEA Online, call 1-800-827-6364 (NEA members should give preferred customer # 0437).

Introduction

"We believe that working on real-world projects connected to the community in some way has more intrinsic educational value than 'time in seat.'"

Gene Bias
High School
Multi-Media Studies
Teacher

Tina Yalen, an eighth grade social studies teacher was teaching her class the major concepts of the American economic system when students began to ask, "Why do we have to know this? How am I going to use this in my life? Why is this important to me?" Clearly, students were not grasping the relevance of their textbook knowledge to their own lives. Yalen also recognized that rote memorization of textbook materials was not promoting true, authentic learning.

So Yalen created a hands-on budgeting project in which students are immersed in life-based experiences that require them to make decisions about money and finances. Her students now "get it" when it comes to economics.

Increasingly, teachers are moving beyond their textbooks, creating lesson plans and curricula that require students to interact with authentic materials found in their community. Authentic materials can be anything from leaves and water streams to interviews with local business owners. In a very real sense, the community becomes the classroom.

When students are required to actually perform tasks and interact with their environment, they learn valuable lessons in problem-solving, decision-making, and responsibility. Hands-on activities encourage students to apply and demonstrate their knowledge and skills in new situations. These are the lessons that stay with students long after the school day ends. These are lessons that foster true, authentic learning.

The six stories in this book demonstrate authentic learning both inside and outside the classroom, using the community as a resource.

The Budget

Tina Yalen no longer hears students question the relevancy of economics principles to real life. Yalen now uses a hands-on budgeting project that gives eighth graders a hefty dose of reality regarding money. Each May eighth graders at Lake Braddock High School assume roles as adults—complete with jobs, incomes, and families. They have apartments to rent, taxes to pay, and budget guidelines to meet.

Building Brotherhood

The Brotherhood School. That's what folks in Kalamazoo, Michigan, dubbed Arcadia Elementary, after the school put on a series of variety shows involving songs, poems, and dances from the many cultures present at the school. The Brotherhood Shows were created as a way to combat ignorance and teach about diversity. Learn how these teachers also integrated lessons in reading, writing, and geography into this program.

History's Best Teachers

Carol Steele, a history teacher at Union High School in Grand Rapids, Michigan, wanted a more authentic approach to teaching history. She wanted to show her students that not all history is learned from textbooks. As a result of Steele's ingenuity, students learned history from the greatest experts of all—those who lived it.

Hands-On Technology

Businesses in Orlando, Florida, are getting technical assistance from an unlikely source. High school students in the multimedia studies program at Edgewater High are putting their computer knowledge to work—literally. Students design animation, logos, and graphics packages for local businesses. In the process, they learn about far more than technology. These students learn how to build teams, meet deadlines, and manage a project from start to finish.

Enterprising Fifth Graders

Enterprise Village is Pinellas County, Florida's hands-on economics program for fifth graders. The mall is stocked with businesses, banks, and restaurants—all operated and managed by students. Parents says it's an eye-opening experience. And students—well, one little girl said it best. On her first day as a banker at Enterprise Village, she stood in the mall wringing her hands. "I'm so nervous," she said. "This is the first time I've been an adult."

Manipulative Math

"Sitting in a chair at a table using a pencil to put marks on a page was not my idea of the best way to teach math readiness skills," says Jeanie Barnett, an elementary school teacher in Madisonville, Kentucky. Barnett embraced Box It Or Bag It, a hands-on math program. Students use authentic materials—from potatoes and popsicle sticks to beans and buttons—to learn a variety of math concepts.

Concluding Thoughts

These stories illustrate there's always a way to reduce "time in seat" and get students interacting with their community. It can be as elaborate as a business arrangement with local companies, or as simple as using household scraps to teach math. Opportunities are ripe in every subject area for hands-on activities that engage students in real, authentic learning.

—Karen Gutloff
Series Editor

Notes:

____

____

____

____

____

MAKING ENDS MEET

These eighth grade teachers threw out their economics textbooks and created a hands-on budgeting project that turns students into expert money managers.

1 Picture this scene. The bell has rung and the students are seated. With calculators and pencils ready and worksheets laid out, they seem like thoroughbreds at the gate awaiting the signal to take off! The scene is even more remarkable because it is happening with only four weeks left in the school year, typically a time when both teachers and students are in the count-down mode. There really is no mystery here, though. You are simply seeing students ready to begin what they have been anxiously awaiting all year. They are starting our personal budgeting simulation, Making Ends Meet, affectionately nicknamed The Budget. This scene has been an annual occurrence at Lake Braddock Secondary School for almost 15 years as part of the economics unit of the eighth grade social studies program.

Our school is located in Burke, Virginia, a suburban middle-class community near Washington, D.C. Lake Braddock is one of the largest schools in the state and has an ethnically diverse student population of about 4,000 students spanning grades seven through 12.

From early May until almost the end of the school year, Lake Braddock's entire eighth grade class of over 650 students is transformed into a group of "budget adults" with randomly selected incomes and lifestyles. The simulation is designed so that all students deal with required family and household expenditures while staying within a given set of guidelines—eventually ending up "in the black."

TINA YALEN
Eighth Grade Social Studies Teacher
MICHAEL MAGATHAN
Eighth Grade Social Studies Teacher

Lake Braddock Secondary School
Burke, Virginia

Learning Connected to the Real World

As veteran teachers, with about a half-century of teaching experience between us, we have seen (as many of you surely have) curricular innovations come and go over the years. Most, thankfully, have gone. But our budget simulation has withstood the test of time, achieving almost legendary status here at Lake Braddock. We believe there is a reason for this. Put simply, our budget project embraces a teaching method that seems to work with middle school students. We use a teaching method that can be applied in any curricular area with a wide variety of subject matter and learning objectives. We simply give students an opportunity to connect their learning to the real world. Our budget simulation is reality based, and the learning is hands-on. The work gets done via a blend of teaching, talking, and teamwork. It balances the middle school students' need to use their imagination and energy while at the same time forcing the students to stay grounded in reality. While focusing on skills for living, the experience packs a sense of adventure our students crave. This translates into the enthusiasm and positive energy that makes the last month of school so satisfying.

The Quest For Genuine Understanding

Understanding the major concepts and forces of the American economic system is one of the major components of the eighth grade social studies program in Fairfax County. We faced a problem, however, as we taught about economics. Our middle school students were not really grasping the relevance of this knowledge to their own lives. All of us as teachers have heard the student cry of "Why do we have to know this? How am I going to use this in my life? Why is this important to me?" We decided these were valid questions that deserved answers. We believed that students needed not only to understand economic principles, but also to be able to put them into practice. Our students' understanding of the subject had to be genuine. We needed "a hook." After all, the students were all of 13 or 14 years old, most with only an allowance for income, and economic needs (and wants) met, in most cases, by others. Furthermore, they seemed to lack any real appreciation of how challenging it was for their parents to meet their needs and wants.

> *All of us as teachers have heard the student cry of "Why do we have to know this? How am I going to use this in my life? Why is this important to me?" We decided these were valid questions that deserved answers.*

Our students' knowledge of budgeting systems meant little, short of enabling them to respond to a set of questions on a test. We decided they needed to be in the system, even if only for a short while in an artificial setting. Maybe then, we thought, some meaningful learning would result. In short, the students needed to become providers for a while instead of receivers.

As you can imagine, there was no need to teach our students how nice it is to have money (the more the better!) or how much fun it is to spend it. To no one's surprise, however, we discovered that most of our students really didn't have a clue about how the adults in their lives make tough money-management decisions each day in order to make ends meet in their households. Our goal was to take them from this darkness into the light! We decided to close this gap and provide a dramatic reality check via a personal budgeting simulation built around cooperative learning. As role players in this simulation, they would have to take on some of the financial responsibilities of adulthood by meeting family and household needs first before any luxury spending could even be considered. Beyond that, they would have to keep all expenses within their income, and matched to their marital and family status.

Gathering Authentic Materials

To truly meet their goals, we asked our students to use authentic resources. Each student had to seek out and learn to use resources usually reserved for adults: tax forms, classified ads, apartment and homeowner directories, real estate ads, nutritional guides, forms from both private and governmental agencies, etc. More important, they would be expected to seek advice from people who make real budgeting decisions every day—their parents and other adults in their lives.

Adjustments and improvements have been ongoing in the evolution of

---

Ten Stages of The Budget

1. Preliminary Activities
   a. Money Management IQ Questionnaire
   b. Series of current articles to read & use, focused on budgeting, cost of living, costs of raising children, the ways real people "make ends meet," particularly at the lower and middle income levels in the U.S.
   c. Worksheet analyzing expenses of a middle class suburban family and how a "typical" family works to meet those expenses
   d. Parent letter and collection of resources

2. Handbook—an overview with rules and regs of the simulation

3. Lottery, Courtship, Weddings

4. Calculation and payment of taxes

5. Calculation of budget guidelines

6. Completion of all eight expenditure worksheets

7. Final calculations for the bottom line

8. Creation of cover, and collating and turning in the Budget Packet

9. Evaluation process

10. Debriefing

this simulation. In the beginning, the two of us used this simulation in our own classes on a very modest scale. Through years of trial and error and reevaluation, it has become an ambitious project involving every eighth grade student and social studies teacher at our school. All 27 eighth grade social studies classes participate in The Budget simultaneously within

> We have seen curriculum innovations come and go over the years. But our budget simulation has withstood the test of time.

their own classrooms. The teachers meet to coordinate planning, timing, and photocopying (and there is lots of that). We continually monitor our progress through the simulation as talk of The Budget permeates our school.

Setting the Stage

In anticipation of The Budget, preparatory work is needed both inside and outside the classroom. Within the classroom we walk our students through several activities to highlight the need for good money management. We illustrate, for example, the concept of budgeting by analyzing various newspaper articles that focus on money management and the costs of living. In addition, students evaluate their own money management IQ using a questionnaire that helps them analyze their shopping/consumer skills. We then bring budget thinking closer by predicting the expenditures that their own families have to deal with (from mortgages to braces). Next, we brainstorm ways families can make ends meet when wants and needs seem unlimited, but incomes are not. We expose them to current data on such subjects as the cost of living, the costs of raising a child from pregnancy through college, the realities of living at or below the poverty line, and the particular challenges of living as a member of America's "middle class" in the 1990s. Finally, we present them with a pie graph that illustrates household expenditures for a family trying to make ends meet.

During this time we also send a letter home to parents both as a courtesy and as a necessity. The Budget project requires students to function in a pretend adulthood for a few weeks, and encourages children to communicate with the adults in their lives about real-life decision-making. For that reason we feel it is important and constructive for parents to be invited into the process. Our budget simulation is not teaching in the traditional sense. It pushes our young teens into adult roles. We have consequently encountered occasional parental concern that we might encourage thinking that marriage is a game. Parents also worry students are too young to have to deal with these kinds of decisions. When concerns like this arise we always respond as quickly as possible to explain our objectives and procedures. In almost all cases the apprehensions disappear. On rare occasions, we make accommodations to ease any anxiety (for example, guaranteeing parents their son or daughter will have a single status).

At this stage, students are encouraged to collect store catalogues, classified ad sections, fliers, home and apartment guides. We also encourage them to collect the food, travel, and entertainment sections of their newspapers as well as other tools that could help them make spending decisions. They must provide proofs of their purchases when they turn in a final project.

Once the stage is set, the simulation begins in earnest. Invariably, despite our efforts to keep students reality based up to this point, their imaginations are generally going wild, with fantasies of Caribbean vacations, lakefront mansions, and luxury automobiles dancing in their heads.Their vision is clouded by swarming dollar signs and their ears are filled with the music of the malls.

Little do they know how soon reality will be setting in. More sober times lay just ahead.

The Action Begins: The Lottery

Once the preparation is behind us, it is time to establish the players and begin the adventure. What better way to start than with a lottery. On that day, every eighth grader learns his or her budget ID, which includes a gross annual income (and sometimes it truly is GROSS!) as well as a marital and parental status. We are careful to point out to our students that our budget lottery is done randomly in the interest of fairness. In real life, one's income and status are often directly related to hard work, preparation, and goal-setting (never miss a chance to teach [preach]). The tension is high because they know ahead of time income options will range from about $26,000 to $55,000, and some will choose single, others married with no kids, and others married with kids. They know that the maximum number of kids is two, with most marrieds

having one or none. They also know that immediately after the lottery they will be offered a 10-minute trading session where they can wheel and

List of Required Budget Expenditures

1. Federal, state, and social security taxes

2. Set expenses (medical/dental, health/life insurance, professional/union dues) and child care costs

3. Miscellaneous expenses (emergencies, household repairs, fines, school fees, holiday and gift expenses, etc.) and savings/donations

4. Housing and utilities (mortgage or rent, electricity, gas, water, phone)

5. Transportation (car note, insurance, maintenance, fuel, fees)

6. Groceries (list built from nutritionally balanced, varied menu), household and personal grooming items

7. Clothing and accessories

8. Home furnishings and appliances

9. Entertainment and recreation (including meals out, hobbies, and vacations)

Decision Time: To Team or Not To Team

Once the lottery and trading session are behind us, the students with a married status are faced with yet another decision. Although the singles must remain single throughout the simulation, the marrieds can choose to go through the simulation as either Married Real (MR) or Married Imaginary (MI). To help with their decison-making, we spend some class time reviewing the advantages and disadvantages of each choice. We point out, for example, that by choosing Married Real, two classmates (spouses) can combine their incomes, have a real live teammate to share work and decision making with, and may get a more vivid sense of the compromise, cooperation, and teamwork involved in marriage. They also would have to combine children so that their expenses would increase. They may need two cars instead of one since both parents would be working outside the home, and decision making may be more challenging than if each had been working alone. To those tempted to marry for money (and there are quite a few of those), we issue a special warning: we don't do Budget divorces! We make sure students understand that once a couple commits to the simulation as Married Reals (MRs), they are committed as a partnership to see the project through to its completion, regardless of claims of incompatibility, mental sufffering, or even infidelity. Parents are informed of this as well. Unfortunately, there are always some students who are so tempted by another's high income or looks that they foolishly disregard any warning signals that this would not be a match made in heaven.

After a 24-hour period of matchmaking (The Courtship), decisions are finalized. Partners declare themselves and a formal Partnership Ceremony (the Wedding) is held, complete with fake flowers and mini-veils, a cooperation/commitment oath, and even wedding portraits as souvenirs for each lovely couple. We've even

deal to try to get the status they want. Some, for example, really want to experience the budget married, but pull a single status in the lottery. They then have 10 minutes to find someone who picked married and make the switch.

had parent-made wedding cakes.

Budgeting Begins

For obvious reasons, we forego the honeymoon and get right to work in classrooms organized into three work zones: a Single Zone, a Married Real Zone, and a Married Imaginary Zone. This arrangement might seem like a three-ring circus to an outsider, but it really is just the opposite as it allows students of similar "lifestyles" to cooperate with and help each other. It also helps us as teachers because we can more easily focus on each lifestyle's special needs as we move from zone to zone. We begin class each day with a review of directions and tasks. We teachers then become "guides on the sides," roaming from zone to zone monitoring progress, answering questions, offering advice, and even providing marriage counseling to troubled MRs. The work takes on a life and pace of its own as each budget adult or couple moves systematically through their spending requirements and tries to stay within expenditure guidelines.

It is always interesting to see how student euphoria over their perceived wealth quickly slides into stunned depression as they pay state, federal, and social security taxes and arrive at the most important calculation of the entire simulation: their net monthly (disposable) income (NMI). By design, this is their first act as "adults" and while it is a sobering moment for them, it is difficult for us not to smile as we watch them take the jolt. Our students then proceed directly to their second step. They take their NMI and, using the recommended guidelines, compute the acceptable expenditure range for each of their eight required expenditures. This set of spending ranges will become their constant reference point as they proceed through the budget-making spending decisions.

After the realities set in, students rebound, of care costs, donations to charity, forced savings, as well as the many high costs of living in the Washington metro area. It is a rude awakening for students as they trade Nordstroms for K-Mart, buy wardrobes without status labels, and drive used or compact cars instead of that BMW of their dreams.

Using the classifieds, students then find a job that matches their budget

While focusing on skills for living, The Budget packs a sense of adventure our students crave.

course, and move on to face basic expenses such as health and life insurance premiums, child- income (though not necessarily their life goals). They must find appropriate and affordable housing—the biggest challenge, and usually below their standards.

They must also buy at least one car and deal with all the expenses connected with car ownership from repairs and gas to license plates and insurance. In addition, the students plan a nutritionally balanced and varied menu

The administration buys into it because it has high student involvement, convincing educational value, and vocal support from parents.

appropriate for their family situation and calculate the costs for all meals and snacks. They must clothe themselves and their children realistically, and provide some furnishings and appliances for their homes. We also remind students that quality of life is an important consideration as well, so we do require that some planning and spending go into recreational and entertainment activities.

Throughout the simulation, students use the catalogues, newspaper sections, classifieds, ad fliers, and guides they have gathered. They make phone calls to local businesses and agencies, go grocery shopping, and actually calculate nutrition and value. They even do comparison shopping for children's clothing. To their dismay, we ask them to perform many mathematical calculations, practice problem-solving constantly, learn to compromise, and make tough decisions (often having to put needs ahead of wants). As a result, the students begin to see their parents in new ways. They start developing an awareness that parents sometimes really do make sacrifices for their children. We believe the students begin to appreciate the ways their own parents have managed to provide for them despite all the demands on parents' incomes. These lessons alone might justify the project, and it is an exciting and rewarding experience to witness their transformations.

The Finale

In the end, after about three weeks of work, each budget adult or couple produces a Budget Packet to turn in, enclosed in a creative cover that visually captures the experience for them. The packet includes an overview page that presents a profile of their budget ID, a completed set of worksheets detailing their tax calculations and their spending decisions for the nine required expenditure categories, a summary page that combines totals and shows the bottom line, and a section for defending any out-of-guideline spending decisions. The packet ends with sheets for peer evaluation, parent evaluation, and teacher evaluation.

Parent, Administrator Buy-In

As this personal budgeting simulation has evolved over the years at Lake Braddock, we have had consistent support from a variety of administrators, enthusiastic involvement by our colleagues, and widespread encouragement from our students and their parents. The adminstration buys into it because it has high student involvement, convincing educational value, vocal support from parents, and reflects well on the school. Parents seem to realize its value in both the short- and long-term learning of their children. Many parents comment in writing as they evaluate their child's budget packet with statements like these: "This has been an excellent real-life project which has taught more than a thousand lectures could ever convey," and "This was a wonderful experience for us and a great 'reality check' for our daughter. I doubt there will be too many complaints in the future about my bargain hunting!" One father went so far as to say, "I could have used this course thirty years ago!" A number of parents have asked (probably only half in jest) if it would be possible for their spouse to go through the simulation!

Most of the teachers involved have also been very positive about the experience. Those who have been with us and moved on to other schools have taken The Budget with them to introduce at their new schools. New colleagues buy into it because they can sense the enthusiasm and commitment from those of us who have made it part of our Lake Braddock life. While they agree that the first time through the simulation can be a daunting experience, we veterans guide them through it, and once it is rolling, they relax and enjoy it along with the rest of us.

As with any major creative project, there are some downsides that anyone considering this program must know. The simulation is very paper intensive. Between the preliminary activities, the handbook of rules and regs, and the workbook for expenditure calculations, we use many reams of paper. In addition, budget work is very high energy due to the many eager questions students have as they work. This is made even more interesting because the students are all moving at their own pace and the teacher has to leap from one mind-set to another as he or she roams from zone to zone (Single, MR, MI) during any given class period. Despite these demands, when it is all said and done, most of us look forward to next year's budget season almost as much as the students do.

Budget No-No's

The goal in this personal budgeting simulation is NOT "to beat the system." Students are not permitted to use any special advantages not available to the public at large. Here are a few examples:

- no free car because you might have found a job that offers it as a perk

- no free food because you happen to work in a restaurant or food service

- no living at home with your parents in a basement apartment in order to avoid paying rent or food costs

- no military careers simply because we want you to have to pay up front for medical/ dental costs and use non-commissary prices for groceries

- no loans from "wealthy classmates"

What Parents Say About The Budget

" This is a real eye-opener for these kids that should give them some appreciation of what their parents go through every day. As extensive as the 'Budget Requirements' are, they just begin to scratch the surface!"

"Excellent exercise. I could have used it thirty years ago."

"This has been an excellent 'real-life' project which has taught more than a thousand lectures could ever convey."

" This is a wonderful experience and a great 'reality check.' I doubt that there will be too many complaints in the future about my bargain hunting! I love it!!"

"Marvelous project idea! A taste of the real world. Wish I could have seen my daughter handle one of those lower incomes with kids. Excellent to see this type of work in the school curriculum."

"It was a great exercise for my daughter to see why we say 'no' to things and why we can't afford some things. She has a new appreciation of all the advantages she has like her dancing lessons etc. It was also an opportunity for us to share with her the funny things we did when we were starting out to make ends meet and how creative you can be to find clothes and entertainment."

"How wonderful to find out in a practical way what a college education will do for you and how valuable good grades and scholarships will be. Even with an education, my daughter now sees that at the entry level, it's still pretty tough out there."

Expanding The Budget

Once the simulation is over, we debrief our students to solicit their feedback and advice, which is often quite insightful. From there, we eighth grade teachers sit down together and make any revisions and updates we want to include for the following year. We have been tinkering with "Making Ends Meet" for years and are always looking for ways to make it as relevant and valuable as possible. For example, some parents and students have suggested we broaden our budget statuses to include single parents next year. Given the recent census data, this would certainly be a very realistic addition. We are also currently looking at ways to blend our budget simulation with the Computer Age. As the availability of computers increases in our school, we are now anticipating using this technology to help the students as they work through the calculations of the budget. Furthermore, as our middle school is now organized around interdisciplinary teams, we are actively pursuing ways to make the simulation an interdisciplinary activity.

We truly believe in the learning merit of this simulation. We have recently made a presentation to the school board about its value as a real-life learning tool. The student member of the school board, currently a senior at Lake Braddock and an alumnus of our budget project went on record saying, " went through The Budget and it is truly an excellent program. My 'wife' did a great job taking care of me!" We have offered to do workshops for our colleagues in the county, sharing with them the procedures and the pitfalls of giving their eighth grade classes the budget experience. It is our dream to one day see every eighth grade student in Fairfax County have the opportunity to survive The Budget!◆

Student Feedback on The Budget

"I learned that I am in no hurry to get married and I may NEVER have any kids!"

"This was awesome! If I could come out in the black on MY lowly income, anyone can do it. I just had to learn to like leftovers, get used to driving an old car, and look hard for free things to do. I was surprised how much there is!"

"No way I could live on that income REALLY. I think I see why my parents keep telling me how important my education is going to be."

"This got frustrating at times. I'm not sure I'm ready to grow up yet."

"Now my Dad wants me to help him do a family budget!"

"Can I get the divorce now? My husband has been driving me crazy. He was so CHEAP."

"My least favorite part was doing the taxes. I really thought I was rich until I had to pay them. I was sure there was a mistake in the tax tables. There wasn't."

"I dread the next time I need another new pair of sneakers. I'm afraid I'll feel guilty about how expensive they are!"

"My parents must be geniuses! I really don't know how they do this!"

Ten Tips on Budget Planning

1 If possible, plan and coordinate the simulation with another teacher.

2 Organize EARLY. Map out a calendar and flow of the simulation and get photocopying done early!

3 Be proactive with parents; send an introductory letter home well before the simulation actually begins.

4 Have students gather resources and set up a storage system starting at least two weeks before the simulation.

5 Prepare a Budget Packet model and mount it, page by page, in correct sequence on a bulletin board for the students to see and refer to.

6 Have the classroom stocked with items like extra pencils, scissors, tape, gluesticks, scrap paper, calculators, classifieds, and catalogues.

7 Once the simulation is underway, orally review all written directions and focus on one expenditure per day to minimize any confusion.

8 Build into your calendar frequent task checkpoints to monitor progress and keep students on task.

9 Use some class time periodically to orally survey the class on their budget decisions as a "reality-check" for all to hear.

10 Most important, get plenty of sleep, eat a hearty breakfast, wear comfortable shoes, keep a calculator in your pocket, and be ready to laugh a lot!

Student Budget Summary

Net Monthly Income _______________

Expenditure	Rec'd % Range	Low $ Amount	High $ Amount	Amount Spent
Childcare/Set Expenses	5-13%	.05 =	.13 =	
Miscellaneous/Savings	2-5%	.02 =	.05 =	
Housing/Utilities	20-30%	.20 =	.30 =	
Transportation	10-20%	.10 =	.20 =	
Groceries/Household/ Grooming	15-23%	.15 =	.23 =	
Clothing/Accessories	6-12%	.06 =	.12 =	
Furniture/Appliances	2-3%	.02 =	.03 =	
Entertainment/Recreation/ Hobbies, Etc.	3-7%	.03 =	.07 =	

Round off all costs to the nearest dollar (.01-.49 = round down; .50-.99 = round up)

Total Spent ________

Summary: Your Net Monthly Income (NMI) = _______________

Minus Your Monthly Expenses = _______________

Equals Your BALANCE at the end of the month = _______________

CERTIFICATE
OF

This Certifies That

____

have faithfully taken the Budget Wedding Oath.

Given at _____________________ ,this _______ day of __________ , 19__.

____________________   ____________________

Insights: ____

____

____

____

____

Actions for Our School (District) to Consider: ____________

____

____

____

____

____

____

____

USING THE PRESENT TO TEACH THE PAST

A textbook could never match the knowledge these high school students gained from oral histories with elderly neighbors.

2 "Every time an old person dies, it's like a library burning down." This quote has always resonated with me. Two years ago it weighed on my mind as I gazed out of the window of my second-floor classroom. Just up the hill, past the tennis courts, sits an eleven-story senior citizens' building called The Grandview Apartments.

As a history teacher, I had formulated two goals in regard to a more authentic approach to teaching history. One of my goals was to help students realize that not all history is learned from textbooks. Real people experience these things, and soon what you've experienced will become someone else's history.

My other goal was to overcome the categorization, divisions, and stereotypes that exist between students and elderly people. I wanted my students to see that the older generation has something to offer as well. Elderly people are not only a source of history, but nice people who should not be written off or avoided.

It's important in teaching American history to get to the present, or at least the students' lifetime. I've often noticed that teachers run out of time just as the curriculum reaches World War II or the Korean War. I wanted my students to get exposed to the whole span of history. And I felt that they should acquire that knowledge from people who had experienced it, not just from books.

I also wanted my students to perform some sort of service as part of their learning during the year. I'd heard of the Foxfire series and had listened to a day-long presentation on implementing service learning, but both seemed complicated

CAROL STEELE

English and History Teacher

Union High School
Grand Rapids, Michigan

and beyond what I could visualize. I knew I would have to choose something small, something I could reasonably hope to do.

Union High

I've been teaching at Union High School, an urban high school with about 1,400 students in Grand Rapids, Michigan, for the last four years. Grand Rapids is the second largest city in Michigan. It has a diversified economy that usually remains fairly stable even during downturns.

Because Union High is the county bilingual center, we have several hundred students from sixteen nations this year, alongside a regular high school program. We are probably more diverse than any other school in western Michigan.

The area surrounding Union High is strongly blue-collar, with many elderly residents and pockets of suburbia.

It is a section of city that traditionally votes against increased public monies for schools even when the rest of the city votes yes. This is one reason most of our staff believe a closer relationship with the community would benefit the school.

One of my goals was to help my students realize that not all history is learned from books.

The Elderly As a Resource

The Grandview Apartments is not a nursing home. It's a federally subsidized housing site for low-income adults. Most residents are retirees in their sixties, seventies, or eighties. A small number have physical handicaps, but most are actively involved in the scheduled activities at the apartments or in volunteer work in the community, or both.

In the spring of 1993, I called The Grandview's manager and told him I wanted to invite some seniors down to my classroom to talk about their memories of World War II. The manager agreed to post a notice on the bulletin board. While I only got one response, that response was spectacular. Mrs. Evelyn Stewart called to volunteer as a speaker while we were studying the 1940s.

When she came, Mrs. Stewart turned out to be a cozy-looking woman with glowing, shoulder-length white hair. She brought a bulging scrapbook that had been assembled by her deceased husband's mother during World War II. Mrs. Stewart also brought typed notes she had prepared for the speech and spent an hour regaling the class with real-life experiences. She even left the scrapbook with us for several weeks to let students have time to browse through it. Since she was a little nervous, Mrs. Stewart also brought an even older lady who sat silently in the back just to offer moral support.

Mrs. Stewart was twelve years old when

Pearl Harbor was bombed by the Japanese in 1941. When she heard the news, she became fearful planes would appear overhead and drop bombs on her. She remembered the crowds of men driving to the recruiting station to sign up. Although she had been a witness to history, the students tended to ask her about things relevant to her own life experiences: Did you have dances back then? What was dating like? How did your husband propose?

As the school year began in the fall of 1993, I had volunteered for a new challenge in teaching. For the first time I was teaching a block of U.S. History and English to tenth graders whom I kept for two successive hours. I wanted to teach so that students would see how learning in the two areas was related.

After my positive experience with one resident of the Grandview, I thought perhaps I could recruit more seniors there and plan a unit on oral history. I decided to contact a district school administrator who coordinates programs for senior citizens. She provided the name of a contact person at the Grandview—Mrs. Ruth Kuntz, the woman who puts together the residents' newsletter.

I contacted Mrs. Kuntz and she agreed to help. Together we selected days and times for the students to meet with the senior citizens in the community room at the complex. Mrs. Kuntz agreed to find ten interested seniors to work with each of my two blocked classes. Since the building is close enough to walk to even in cold weather, logistics were simple. All I needed were permission slips from parents so that students could leave the school grounds.

I decided three visits on successive weeks would be long enough to form a relationship, and short enough that if I fell on my face and the unit failed, none of us would be committed for a really long period. I developed a long list of questions for each visit, but told students they were free to follow their own conversations. The questions were a backup, in case it was hard for students to think of what to ask.

Hot Chocolate to The Rescue

The students were not enthusiastic when they first heard about the plan. There was some groaning

and a number of cool stares as I explained. We explored stereotypes of elderly people in our English classes by brainstorming words and listing them on the blackboard; the list was weighted heavily toward negatives.

Still, on the appointed day, we trudged up the hill in absolutely frigid temperatures and cautiously entered the apartment building. I had divided the students into groups of three or four so that each small group could meet one of the ten senior citizens I hoped would be waiting for us there. When we got inside, students flocked over to the urn of hot chocolate their hosts had ready for them and began to warm up to the idea of interviewing.

Some senior citizens arrived late, but Mrs. Kuntz finally rounded them all up, including Mrs. Stewart, whom I'd met the previous year. The students spent about seventy-five minutes talking as I circulated among groups; then we went back to the classroom in time for the bell that ends second hour. My afternoon block went on a different day and met with another group of ten adults whom they interviewed.

The schedule was the same for each of the three interview days. The students' attitudes quickly changed, progressing from negative or neutral to positive or enthusiastic. They got to know individual elders and began to enjoy themselves.

The students got a lot more social history and daily life history than they would've gotten from books. Through the interviews, they saw how life affected people forty or fifty years ago. They also changed attitudes. At first, getting them to go to Grandview was like getting them to go for oral surgery. But by the second or third visit, students would say things like "Our lady is so cute!" or "I can't wait to get over there!"

Because of illness or schedule conflicts, not all the seniors could keep coming. Sometimes Mrs. Kuntz found replacements; other times we put more students with the available adults. In some cases the groups began to bond; seniors greeted us at the door with "Where are my boys?" or "Aren't Tiffany and Kara here?" Even in other groups a level of cordiality was soon reached.

By week two, the students were admitting that their experience at the Grandview was not at all what they had expected. They found the senior citizens both interesting and likable. On the last of our scheduled three meetings, right after our requested rendition of the school fight song (demanded by senior citizen alumnae of Union), I found myself promising that we would come back after we had done our oral history reports so that the senior citizens could see the work the students produced.

Oral History Writing Assignments

Back in the classroom, students could choose to do either a report or a piece of historical fiction based on the stories they'd heard. Illustrations were required. The work was generally good and about equally divided between the two approaches. Unfortunately, students don't get enough experience writing to get better at it. Even worse, their

> *The students got a lot more social history and daily life history than they would've gotten from books.*

writing assignments often consist of regurgitating material. But here they were writing about things that felt real, in contrast to ordinary writing assignments.

During one of our visits, Mrs. Stewart heard the students talking about plays they were writing for me in English class and proposed an idea. Could our students perform a play for the seniors at one of their monthly "theatre luncheons"? These consisted of a short play and a big potluck meal.) I agreed that we would try. Mrs. Stewart suggested that the students could read and share their history reports during the same session.

Lights, Camera, Interview!

As my students and I prepared, I got another call from Mrs. Stewart. Now the senior citizens were wondering if our students could participate in an intergenerational TV show. The Retired Senior Volunteer Program produces and broadcasts a weekly show on the public-access channel in Grand Rapids. I agreed to help work it out.

First, three students attended the open house scheduled at the TV station. Then we talked over the opportunity in class and the students expressed interest. We brainstormed long lists of questions we could ask of senior citizens on the first broadcast and questions we'd like them to ask us during the second one.

Intriguing questions arose during this planning. For instance, could we ask elderly people about euthanasia and assisted suicide? On the one hand, it would be enlightening to find out their views; on the other, such questions might be considered indelicate. This issue was resolved by including the question and asking the producer, Sarah Lowe, herself a senior citizen, to screen the questions and delete any she deemed inappropriate.

On the appointed afternoon, I used the school station wagon to transport eight students to Channel 23 in Wyoming, Michigan, a suburb about twenty minutes from our school. The two half-hour TV shows were taped back-to-back. We were there nearly three hours.

Naturally, the students were nervous at first, but after a few minutes in the lounge getting introduced to senior citizens and the pop machine, they began to loosen up. They also got a quick tour of the equipment and the control room before taping began. It took about half an hour just to get everyone seated and get the lights, equipment, microphones, and sound levels prepared for taping. Each student's first response in the panel discussions was a bit stiff, but I was surprised at how quickly they forgot the cameras and focused on the interchanges between seniors and students. They covered a wide range of subjects as the cameras rolled.

The tapes were scheduled for broadcasting during our spring vacation and the following week. But Mrs. Stewart, who always seems to think of everything, arranged for extra copies to be dubbed for the school and for any student who provided a tape. After spring vacation, we took time in class to view both programs. There was some ribbing of students whose mannerisms were captured by the camera but also a strong interest among all members of the two classes, whether they had appeared on tape or not.

The senior citizens were delighted by their intergenerational pro-

grams, so delighted that they requested another such series for next fall.

Our last activity with the residents of the Grandview was the theater luncheon put on by each of the two groups. The morning class went in late April and the afternoon group in early May. Each group presented a play or skit, then read some of the oral history projects, and left the originals with the senior citizens who had inspired them. The senior citizens brought casseroles and salads and all sorts of other goodies. The students brought desserts. The spread of food was a feast, and the camaraderie between young and old was wonderful.

Looking back, I'm surprised at how simple the project was. I really expected it to take more time and effort on my part than it did. The senior citizens were energetic and eager to help and easily fitted our visits into existing systems. For instance, they recruited other Grandview residents to be interviewed through their building newsletter and later simply plugged us into the TV series.

Assessing Growth

The change in the students was quite noticeable. They were reluctant to go at first, but once they tried it they liked it. Most set aside their prejudices, finding the senior citizens likable and not at all depressing. Most also recommended that I repeat the project next year because it was so interesting and different. Feedback from parents and administration was quite positive.

The Authentic Materials Approach

What's unique about authentic learning as applied to my students? It's interactive, for one thing. A student asks a question, gets the answer, and then can ask another question. Or the student can take a new tack, for example, asking about the meaning of a particular word. A book may have a paragraph on the whaling industry, but with an authentic-learning approach you're able to talk to someone who spent years involved first-hand with something like that, and you're sure to get more than a paragraph's worth of memorable information.

Probably the best testinonial to the success of our authentic-learning experience came from the senior citizens themselves. They were absolutely delighted by every visit by the young people. They had hot chocolate waiting in the winter and punch in the spring. The kids basked in their warmth and formed new opinions of aging in America. From a political point of view, maybe increased contact with the young will create a greater willingness among retirees in our area to support school-funding issues.

Now that I know how easily we can work with the seniors who live just up the hill, I'm sure I'll include interactions between them and my students every year. I will definitely do an oral history project next year, but something tells me we'll dream up new variations and additions as we go along.◆

Oral History Report Options

*(These options were given to students writing oral history reports on their
interviews with elderly residents at Grandview Apartments.)*

You may choose one of the options below as you prepare your report based on the interviews at Grandview apartments. Whichever one you choose, be sure to include credits or acknowledgments to the people who provide you with information.

A. Historical Fiction - You may take the information you gathered and create a story from it, like an illustrated children's story book. You might re-combine the facts from one person or use facts from several people as long as the story remains a truthful representation of the era you are describing (the result might be like Laura Ingalls Wilder's books or entirely your own approach).

B. Nonfiction Account - Here you must report the information with complete accuracy, checking facts with other sources such as encyclopedias when you need to verify something. In this approach, you will quote individuals who provide unusual anecdotes or personal outlooks that are used in your report.

Suggested Questions for Oral History Interviews

As we travel to Grandview, remember that you represent Union High School. Please be courteous. Take the first few minutes of your time to introduce the members of the group briefly. You may ask any appropriate question to find out about your elder's early life. The questions below are suggestions you may turn to if you run out of ideas:

1. Where did you grow up? What was it like there?

2. Tell us about the members of your family.

3. What are your earliest memories?

4. Describe a typical school day in your elementary school.

5. What did you study?

6. What was the school room like?

7. How did you get to school?

8. What games and activities did you take part in as a child?

9. Describe your chores and family responsibilities while growing up.

10. Describe your family's holiday observances: Fourth of July, Christmas, Easter or Passover, Thanksgiving, etc.

11. Were birthdays celebrated in your home?

12. Describe your parents' jobs and family responsibilities.

Continued

Suggested Questions for Oral History Interviews
(*Continued*)

13. Did your family can foods, butcher meat, make soap, or do other tasks that aren't usually done at home today? Tell us how.

14. What religious customs, if any, did your family have?

15. What was your normal clothing as a child or teenager?

16. When and how did you get new clothes or shoes?

17. What was teenage social life like when you were in high school?

18. What behavior was required or expected that is different from today? How was politeness defined then?

19. What were your favorite activities or places to go?

20. What was your house like? How did you get around?

21. Tell us about your first job.

22. Describe some historic events you recall. (Pearl Harbor, Great Depression, Korean Conflict)

23. If you married, how did you meet your spouse? What was your wedding like?

24. What relatives were important to you or close to you? Can you tell us some of the stories they told you or things you did together?

25. What about your own children or nieces, nephews, etc. How did you go about raising them?

26. What advice would you give to modern teens?

Reader Reflections

Insights: ____

____

____

____

____

Actions for Our School (District) to Consider: ______________

____

____

____

____

____

____

____

ENTERPRISE VILLAGE

Enterprise Village is the world's only freestanding economics education center for elementary school students.

3

On the surface, Enterprise Village looks like a typical shopping mall. Store owners bustle about preparing merchandise and stocking shelves. Cash registers clang as clerks ring up purchases for lines of shoppers. Bookkeepers furiously write payroll checks. Tellers in the mall's bank cash and deposit payroll checks. Tired shoppers gather at McDonald's and other eateries, their purchases stacked around them.

Look closer and you see what makes this mall stand out. The store owners, clerks, bookkeepers, tellers, and shoppers are all fifth grade students. These students operate Enterprise Village, a hands-on economics education project of the Pinellas County, Florida, school system.

One of the most populous counties in the United States, Pinellas occupies a peninsula that is bordered on one side by Tampa Bay and on the other by the Gulf of Mexico. Our student population of 100,043 makes the system the seventh largest among Florida's sixty-seven counties and the twenty-second largest out of more than 16,000 school districts in the United States.

I am a resource teacher at Enterprise Village. Prior to accepting my current position, I had the great fortune to teach fifth-grade social studies for almost twelve years. I say I was fortunate because our district's social studies department has always been an innovator in the field of economic education. During the late 1980s, we were identified as one of five exemplary K-12 economic education programs in the nation. We have also received more awards in the International Paper Company–Joint Council on Economic Education national competition than any state or district in the na-

SHARON HALL
Resource Teacher
Enterprise Village
Pinellas County, Florida

tion. Also, test results of all fifth-grade students since 1981 show that Pinellas students consistently average above 80 percent on a test of economics knowledge. In grades three, five, and eight, our students average five points above the national norm on items related to economics on the CTBS Achievement Test. Enterprise Village is a continuation of this fan-

Students would expand their knowledge of economics beyond the classroom and actually practice what they are learning.

tastic economic education curriculum. I'm proud to be a part of this world-class economics education program that gives fifth graders in Pinellas County Schools a hands-on learning experience in America's free-enterprise system.

How We Got Started

In 1983 Dr. Howard Hinesley, our present superintendent of schools who was then associate superintendent, returned from a meeting in Kansas City, Missouri, and excitedly described a student-operated economic mini-city he had visited. The project, "Exchange City," was located in a warehouse owned by Hallmark and served fifth and sixth graders from several small school districts. Dr. Hinesley suggested the concept would be an ideal addition to the award-winning program of economic education in Pinel-

las County. Our Social Studies Director Jeanne Freeze, several school board members, and others traveled to Kansas City for a look. They quickly agreed that a project like this would be the perfect culmination of our fifth-grade study of free-enterprise and consumer economics education. Students would be able to expand their knowledge of economics beyond the classroom and actually practice what they were learning.

Our superintendent at the time, Dr. Scott Rose, a vocal advocate of free enterprise, responded immediately by including the development of Enterprise Village as a Superintendent's Priority Objective to be accomplished by 1988. Curriculum had to be written and a facility needed to be built. The

program was about to take off!

Business leaders were contacted by the Pinellas County Education Foundation and its president, Gus Stavros, a dynamic and successful entrepreneur known statewide for his commitment to education. Since public funds could not be used for construction of the facility, major businesses were invited to contribute a minimum of $50,000 each toward construction of the 18,000-square-foot facility. This $50,000 contribution would give the business exclusive rights to a storefront at the Village. Many businesses eagerly committed to support the project. The school board agreed to provide land, staff, supplies, curriculum, and transportation. A local contractor, Leslie A. Rubin, a strong comnunity supporter of economic programs, agreed to construct the building at cost. It quickly became obvious that this project would not remain a dream but would actually become a reality. The community support was there. The school board voted to go forward.

Philosophy and Goals

Approximately 12,000 students, mostly fifth graders, visit Enterprise Village during each school year to learn first-hand what it's like to operate a business. The Enterprise Village project is based on the belief that:

- Economic education is essential preparation for citizenship.
- Students develop a "real" understanding of concepts and skills by following classroom instruction with hands-on involvement in operating a mini-business.
3. A sense of responsibility and a positive attitude toward the free-enterprise system are desirable outcomes.
4. Assistance of sponsors as consultants in program and facility planning is desirable.

Enterprise Village aims to promote student understanding of the free-enterprise system through the following subgoals:
1. develop understanding of the interdependence of producers and consumers;
2. explore the relationship between labor and income;
3. develop understanding of the need for a monetary exchange;
4. make economic choices regarding time, money, and material resources;
5. apply knowledge of K-5 economics concepts in a business simulation; and
6. demonstrate a positive attitude toward the free-enterprise system.

Getting Businesses On Board

With the goals in mind, and community support actively coming forward, Enterprise Village's opening was set for 1989.

The first step involved the hiring of personnel. In June 1987, Keith Gall, a former elementary school teacher, assistant principal, and principal, was hired as manager. Keith sought further business commitments, spearheaded the construction of the facility, and hired three teachers who would join him on the curriculum-writing committee. Having served on curriculum-writing teams prior to this project, I applied for the position and was selected in January 1988 as one of the three resource teachers.

We began by studying the Exchange City project as well as several other economics education prototypes around the country. We then decided to develop our own unique facility and curriculum, to be known as Enterprise Village. The curriculum writing took nearly a year. When completed, the curriculum consisted of eleven economics objectives. They included learning about banking services; learning the skills needed to maintain a checking account; recognizing that career choices are related to personal interest, skills, and a knowledge of job responsibilities; and learning the importance of ethics, teamwork, and decision-making in the operation of a quality business. Simulations were developed for the 100 or more job positions in the Village businesses. Meanwhile, supporting businesses were still coming aboard.

They included to name a few, Barnett Bank, Florida Power, Eckerd Drugs, McDonald's, GTE, AT&T Paradyne, Paragon Cable, Q105 radio, Century 21, Browning-Ferris Industries, Blockbuster Video, and the Pinellas County Water System. What started as a much smaller project was now going to be an 18,000-square-foot facility costing $1.5 million.

Moving Day

The pilot curriculum was completed, printed, and in the hands of teachers. An initial group of nine schools began to study the eight-week unit in February 1989, with the first school scheduled to visit the Village in May. We were getting a little panicky, however, because the construction project was running behind schedule. We finally moved in just two weeks before the first scheduled visit! This meant moving into a huge, empty building with seventeen businesses to furnish from the floor up. Needless to say, the staff worked night and day, but what fun! To see this dreamed-about mini-city come alive was thrilling. As we furnished each office, hung each clock, stocked McDonald's, and prepared the bank, we grew more excited about the first school's visit.

The pilot schools' visits enabled us to see student reaction to the project and their performance. It also allowed us to see where changes were necessary. We spent the summer of 1989 rewriting and reworking the curriculum. I was reprinted and our first full year of operation began that September.

A Typical Day at Enterprise Village

On a typical day at Enterprise Village, the students arrive on school buses dressed for a successful day on the job. During the previous eight weeks they have been preparing for this day. Students have had the opportunity to apply for jobs, be assigned to positions, learn how to write checks and make deposits, and make plans for their business expenses. They are ready to become both business leaders and consumers for one day. They gather in Stavros Square for a final

Enterprise Village is the only freestanding economics education center for elementary school students in the world.

riefing before reporting o work.

Shop Set-Up Time

The first thirty-five minutes of the day is called Shop Set-up Time." There's much to be done before the business is actually ready to open. During this period, the new "employees" work closely with an adult volunteer to organize and plan their day. Although some jobs require the employees to leave the business to do their job, no one actually goes out during set-up time. Rather, students begin preparing paperwork or pricing products that will be sold to customers during the day.

One employee takes a five-dollar check to the warehouse to purchase necessary supplies. The manager prepares to go to

Barnett Bank with a business loan application and promissory note. The bookkeeper begins writing employee payroll checks, while sales clerks learn how to operate computers and other equipment.

Students as Consumers and Employees

At the completion of set-up time, the national anthem is played, signaling the actual opening of the business day. Since all students assume roles as consumers, as well as employees, a series of breaks now begins. Three times during the day, each employee receives a paycheck and goes on a break. (Managers are paid six dollars at each break, bookkeepers receive five dollars, and everyone else is paid five dollars per

pay period.) At any one time, one-third of a business's employees are on break while two-thirds of the employees remain at work running the business. Barnett Bank is the students' first stop. There, students make deposits into their own personal checking accounts. They then become consumers, using the rest of their break time to shop.

Just as in the real world, bank deposits are entered into computers when students visit the teller. When students go to a business and purchase an item, the cashier determines if the student has sufficient funds on account before allowing the purchase to be completed. This requires students to manage their checkbook registers very carefully. If they do not have enough money to make the pur-

chase, the computer says "Purchase Denied."

As a consumer, each student deals with choices about time and money. Since the three breaks are only ten, twenty, and twenty-five minutes long, time is of the essence. Not only can students shop in order to keep the circular flow of the Village economy moving, but they can purchase snacks at McDonald's, and lunch must be eaten. Other activities available to students during their break time include a trip to Morton Plant Hospital for a wellness checkup, a visit to the Community Art Center, a stop at City Hall to vote, or a trip to Browning-Ferris Industries to see an exhibit of recycled items. Making these decisions about time and money really keeps the students thinking!

State-of-the-Village Report

As the day winds down, production and sales cease, rent and utilities have been paid, business loans hopefully have been repaid with interest, and businesses are prepared to give a report at the Town Meeting. Students reconvene in the Village Square to hear a State-of-the-Village address from their mayor. Each business bookkeeper gives a report, as well as the United Way Director, the Water Conservation Specialist, the Bank Savings Officer, and the Attorney-at-Law, who will report on two cases studied during the day. The Quality Business of the Day Award (selected by surveying the student population) is presented, successful businesses are recognized, and commendable business practices are praised.

Back in the Classroom

The day at Enterprise Village ends, but learning does not. The students return to their classroom, where they study the results of their Village visit. A rubric created before the visit is used to evaluate a business's performance as measured against expectations. Was the business successful? Did it make a profit? Why, or why not? How did each student do with his or her checking account? Finally, students study the circular flow of money both at the Village and in the real world. They are also asked to plan a business of their own using concepts they have learned in the Enterprise Village unit of study.

Parent Volunteers

Not only are students and teachers excited about the Enterprise Village experience, but parents, who become actively involved, also love it. The program requires that each Village business have at least one adult volunteer working with the students during their day. Prior to the Village visit, teachers recruit parents, grandparents, or friends to attend a two-and-a-half hour volunteer-training session at the Village. Following this training, the adults come along and serve as shop supervisors. Parents answer questions, help students stay on schedule, assist students in preparing for their breaks, and help as students make entries into their checkbook registers. It is not uncommon to hear parents sometimes say they are more nervous than their children.

Program Evaluation

We've evaluated Enterprise Village in several ways. Teachers give pre- and post-tests, which accompany the curriculum. The post-test scores show dramatic improvement in student knowledge of economics issues. The results from a testing of eighth grade students further as-sures us our program has a lasting impact. We oper-ate a summer program for seventh-, eighth-, and ninth-grade students called Business Leaders 2000. A pre-test was ad-ministered to chart the re-tention of those students who had attended Enter-prise Village in grade five. We compared their test re-sults with those of stu-dents who had not stud-ied the Village curriculum earlier. Again, the results verified that our students knew more about econom-ics than those who had not gone through the cur-riculum.

The evaluation we en-joy the most, however, is the response from teach-ers, parents, and students. Teachers are a bit nervous when they teach the cur-riculum for the first time but are thrilled by the time the experience is over. Nearly all agree that it's a curriculum that they love to teach because of the student reaction and their belief in a hands-on approach.

Parents leave after their day at the Village exhaust-ed but in awe of what they've seen the students do. Some of them say things like "I don't recog-nize this as my child. It's a side of them that I don't see at home. We need this program for two days in-stead of one." Another statement commonly heard from parents is "Please, we need a pro-gram like this in middle school or high school. We'd love our children to get a second dose."

But watching and lis-tening to the students pro-vides the best evaluation of all. Many feel so re-sponsible as they perform their duties that they don't want to relinquish any of their time to go on break: "I can't leave. I have too much work to get done." Watching students cooperate, work as a team with one goal in mind, and perform successfully in their business, is a thrill beyond words for a teacher. Discipline prob-lems are nearly nonexis-tent in Enterprise Village.

Future Plans

During the 1994-95 school year, we began examining the possibility of program and facility expansion. Our goal is to develop programming that will al-low middle and high school students the op-portunity to have a fol-low-up to their fifth-grade experience. The middle school summer program, Business Leaders 2000, has shown us that stu-

dents are very interested in carrying on this learn-ing experience. Over the past two years, we have had to turn down hun-dreds of students interest-ed in spending five weeks of their summer vacation

What Students Say About Enterprise Village

"Enterprise Village was an experience of a lifetime. It was like a regular shopping mall. I learned that if you set prices too low, you go out of business quickly."

"I enjoyed Enterprise Village so much. I'd do anything to go again! I learned so much about Kane's Furniture (because I worked there). I think I'll work there when I grow up."

"Enterprise Village is a smash! It was weird being in adult shoes for a day. I didn't think the stores would be so elaborate. It was awesome to learn what an adult does every day."

"I just came back from Enterprise Village and loved it. Being a bookkeeper at Eckerd's was hard but it suited me. I had one of the best days of my life. I also learned how to write checks and make deposits."

"While I was at Enterprise Village, I learned how much adults do to provide for themselves and their families. I also learned how managers of stores feel frustrated at times."

studying economics education. We hope to have some plans in action within the next two years.

We are also working with other school districts throughout the state of Florida and around the United States to develop similar programs. There are many ways to implement this type of programming among all levels of students without having the million-dollar facility to experience and put into action concepts that they are learning in the classroom.

For Advice on Starting Your Own Enterprise Program, contact Enterprise Village at 12100 Starkey Rd., Largo, FL 34643 (813) 588-3746.◆

A little girl stood in front of the bank,
wringing her hands, and saying,
"I'm so nervous, this is the first time I've been
an adult."

that we are so fortunate to have in Pinellas County. The bottom line is that students have the chance

Enterprise Village Desired Student Outcomes

1 Relate *ECONOMIC TERMS* to *BUSINESSES* represented at Enterprise Village: goods, services, needs, wants, producer, product, production, free enterprise, competition, profit, nonprofit, opportunity cost, public property, and private property.

2 Recognize some methods a *QUALITY BUSINESS* uses to collect data so it can continue to improve.

3 Demonstrate the skills involved in maintaining a *CHECKING ACCOUNT*: depositing payroll checks, writing personal checks, maintaining a check register.

4 Identify *BANK SERVICES* and relate them to businesses and consumers at Enterprise Village.

5 Recognize that *CAREER/JOB CHOICE* is related to personal interest, skills, and knowledge of job responsibilities.

6 Recognize the importance of *ETHICS*, *TEAMWORK*, and *DECISION MAKIN*G in the operation of a quality business.

7 Identify *INDIVIDUAL JOB RESPONSIBILITIES* of employees at Enterprise Village.

8 Identify *RESPONSIBILITIES* of a *QUALITY BUSINESS*.

9 Make *BUSINESS DECISIONS* in preparation for your day at Enterprise Village.

10 Complete necessary *PROCEDURES* in preparation for your day at Enterprise Village.

11 Describe the *CIRCULAR FLOW* of goods, services, labor, and money between households and businesses at Enterprise Village.

Create A Business

Work with a partner, or alone, to create a new business. Complete the following business plan for your new business.

Type of Business ____

Name of Business ____

Job Titles	Job Responsibilities
______________________	______________________
______________________	______________________
______________________	______________________
______________________	______________________

List the goods or services the business would produce. How much would you charge for each one?

Goods or Services	Price
______________________	__________
______________________	__________
______________________	__________

Continued

Create A Business (*Continued*)

What materials will you need?

____

____

____

Who would want to shop in this store?

____

____

How would you get people to shop in this store?

____

____

What would you do if your store did not have enough customers?

____

____

____

Student Activities at Enterprise Village

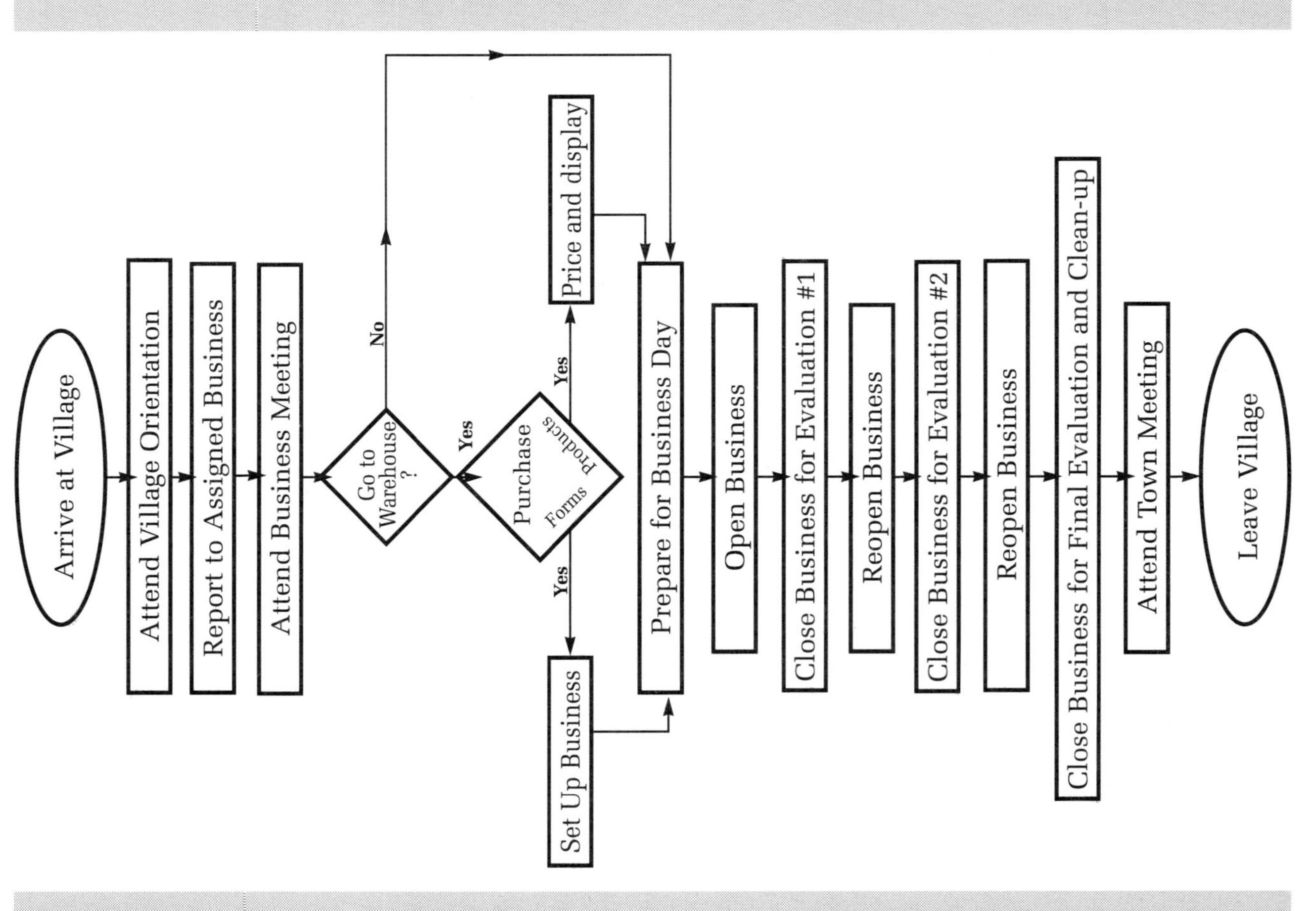

Insights: ____

____

____

____

____

Actions for Our School (District) to Consider: ____________________

____

____

____

____

____

____

THE BROTHERHOOD SCHOOL

Here's how a multicultural variety show helped teach students, parents, and teachers about diversity.

4 Located in southwestern Michigan, the city of Kalamazoo has a population of about 80,000. According to the *Kalamazoo Gazette*, "The people of Kalamazoo County are almost a perfect microcosm of the 'salad bowl' society developing in America."

Several factors contribute to Kalamazoo's diversity. The community's colleges and universities recruit international students and families. Globally oriented businesses such as the Upjohn Company, which has its world headquarters in Kalamazoo, attract professionals from many countries. The area is a regional medical center, and offers an exceptional range of services to people with disabilities. This part of Michigan is also the occasional home of a number of migrant workers. Not surprisingly, the student population of the school district accurately reflects this "salad bowl society."

The Kalamazoo School District has about 12,000 students. It is the largest district in Kalamazoo County and is racially, economically, and ethnically diverse. Students speak at least one of forty-four languages ranging from Abud to Zulu.

DOLORES DONOHUE
MONICA MARTINEZ RYBARCZYK

Arcadia Elementary School
Kalamazoo, Michigan

Diversity at Arcadia Elementary

A 1972 court-ordered desegregation plan ensured a racially diverse student population, beginning in the 1980-81 school year. Arcadia Elementary School in Kalamazoo housed three bilingual (Spanish/English) classrooms—one classroom for students with emotional impairments, and another for educable children with mental impairments. This was significant because the school contained only thirteen classrooms as a "lower elementary" building for grades K-3. Children from affluent families attended Arcadia, as did children of migrant workers and the sons and daughters of many international students at nearby Western Michigan University. Each class at Arcadia had some students who did not speak English. Clearly, the school represented the whole wide world.

Despite the diversity of the student population,

ignorance was sometimes displayed by students, parents, school staff, and community members. One school administrator referred to the "different clientele" at the school. While calling roll, one teacher pronounced "Jose'" as "Josie," embarrassing the student and causing him to be teased at recess. Many people did not realize that almost all of the students in the bilingual classrooms were

born in the United States; the students were continually being asked what country they were from. Arabic students, fasting for Ramadan, were thought to be sick or were encouraged to eat all of their lunch. Some students in special education were avoided because of certain mannerisms they demonstrated. Some parents referred to other parents who were different in some way from them as "those people." Community members remarked about the "disadvantages," "problems," and "overwhelming odds" at the school.

Actually, the school was quite good. However, everyone needed to be given more knowledge about the diverse population in our school. Errors in communication had to be corrected in a positive way.

The Brotherhood Show

In order to unite the diverse student body and to eliminate ignorance, we decided to "put on a show!"—one that would educate students and faculty about the many different cultures present in our school. We saw this as a hands-on way to teach about diversity. We also realized that students sometimes learn better by participating in an activity than by reading a book. We developed a stage program during the 1980-81 school year with the children as stars, and called it the "Brotherhood Show." A different program, with the theme of brotherhood, was presented annually on the school stage each February from 1981 to 1991. Each program was written specifically for the students involved. The

> *To unite the diverse student body and to eliminate ignorance, we decided to "put on a show!"—one that would educate students and faculty about the many different cultures present in our school.*

programs showcased the multiethnicity and special abilities of the students, while promoting values of brotherhood, self-esteem, pride in one's heritage, pride in the United States, and the value of global communication. The media for this message was songs, poetry, dance, drama, humor, visual displays, crafts, and tradiional clothing from around the world. Much of each program was in languages other than English.

Through the Brotherhood Shows, students learned to appreciate one another as members of many societies. This is both a regional and national issue, as well as an educational goal. The shows provided a wonderful opportunity for home and community involvement.

Parents and guardians were active participants along with grandparents, relatives, and friends. Parents requested certain artistic modes, provided their own authentic materials, and became resource teachers. At home, family discussions focused on the program. There was an atmosphere of creative, cooperative learning by young and old. This was something done not only *for* multiethnic, multiabled, multilingual, and multicultural children and adults, but *by* them. Assimilation used to mean incorporating people from all over the world into our society. Through the Brotherhood Shows, assimilation was presented as a way of incorporating people of diverse backgrounds and abilities into a society in which multiple language skills, and ability levels are recognized as assets. Additionally, the shows brought together—in a positive way—people who otherwise might not have met.

Brotherhood in Action

The first program was performed by students in the three bilingual classrooms (students in these classrooms formed the core group of each show thereafter). The program was a small but resounding success. Because the bilingual classes had students from many racial and ethnic groups, it was thrilling to see them promote the values of the Brotherhood Shows together. Subsequent programs included students from other Arcadia classrooms, bilingual and academically talented students from different schools, and Arcadia's

special-education students.

One year, a first-grade class, second-grade class, and class for students with emotional impairments, combined to form one act. They worked and rehearsed together, and we observed that they also played together more at recess. Among other routines, the students sang the song "Fifty Nifty," which lists all fifty states in alphabetical order. They recited a poem naming the nine planets in order of their distance from the sun while giving the characteristics of each planet. They tied this to the theme of brotherhood by emphasizing that we all

African-American leaders. The students had used their library skills, reading skills, and language arts skills to research, write, and present the reports.

The students from the educable mentally impaired (EMI) class performed a maypole dance with a third-grade class.

in human ability. They developed a buddy system with the other students and the maypole dance was performed so smoothly that few in the audience knew which students were from the special-education class. Meanwhile, the students from the EMI class mastered physical coordination objectives.

In another show, first grade teacher Dolores Vasquez watched with pride as her students sang a song in Spanish that Vasquez's mother had sung to her as a child. They played the game London Bridge in English, Spanish, and Malay, and ended their act with the Mexican dance "La Raspa."

bilingual teacher Hanh Ha worked with a mother from Laos. The mother was teaching a traditional Laotian dance to three Laotian girls—one kindergartner and two first-graders. Ha is trilingual—she speaks Vietnamese, French, and English. The mother spoke only Lao. Somehow, Ha and the mother communicated and this act was put together. The mother also sewed the girls' clothing for this dance.

Majida Albkower was a mother who contacted all the Arabic-speaking parents, held rehearsals in her home, and came to school on a weekly basis to rehearse the students. Before returning to Jordan that June, Mrs. Albkower told us one of the highlights of the family's stay in the United States was the Brotherhood Show

> *All students are at the beginning of a spectrum—they are learning about their places in society.*
> *At the other end of the spectrum, they will assume their leadership roles and teach others to follow in their footsteps.*

live together in this nation, this world, this universe.

One act presented dramatized reports on

While the third-graders easily learned the dance, they also learned to respect and appreciate differences

Parent Enthusiasm And Involvement

Parents were an integral part of our Brotherhood Shows. For one show,

Mrs. Albkower felt that she was needed, wanted, and appreciated. She was glad that her family's language and culture received such respect from the educational system.

Because of the friendships made during one Brotherhood Show, many community members were invited to a traditional Malaysian wedding. During the reception, a Malaysian mother spoke of her fears, anxieties, and hopes for her family in the United States. She said that they were here for only three years while she and her husband studied for master's degrees. Her fears that her children would have difficulty in school were allayed by caring teachers and students who practiced brotherhood. Her anxieties that her children would lose their cultural identity changed when she was contacted and asked to participate in the Brotherhood Show. The mother taught the Malaysian dance "Kain Pelikat" for that show. Because of her involvement, she regularly visited her children's school, came to know the teachers very well, formed friendships with other parents, and shared part of the Malaysian culture with everyone.

Although we started out small for the original show, experience and planning helped us to grow each year. Per program, the minimum number of participating children was 103; the maximum was 301. Each child drew approximately five adults as audience members. A core group of six teachers and one principal planned each show, but at least forty-five more teachers, administrators, paraprofessionals, family, and community members came to be involved in the programs.

Community Participation

Former Kalamazoo mayor and community leader Francis P. Hamilton became the "guardian angel" of each show. He donated personal funds and called upon his network of business leaders to get us everything from bleachers to tap shoes. He was also instrumental in gaining outside funding for the shows.

By invitation, we took the shows "on the road" to Western Michigan University, city festivals, senior citizen centers, state educational conferences, and the Rotary International Club of Kalamazoo.

Kalamazoo high school students who operated the student-run broadcasting station, videotaped the shows for broadcast on community-access television.

Applications To Classroom Learning

Community members—many of whom would have had little or no contact with the school system otherwise—received and responded to personal, handwritten invitations from students (a painstaking task for the young children). For each letter that met the qualifications of neatness, legibility, and correct spelling, the student received a Hershey's kiss. Because each student wrote at least three letters of invitation, students acquired letter-writing skills (which are tested in the Metropolitan Achievement Test), reinforcement of English-language skills, and effective communication skills. Students had to write three letters of invitation in school over a three-week period. They could write as many letters as they wanted at home and collect a Hershey's kiss for each letter handed in. One year, a student wrote

Mrs. Albkower was glad that her family's language and culture received such respect from the educational system.

forty-two letters of invitation. We were afraid her dentist would be writing to us!

Mail Call

The invitations were mailed in January, a month before the show. Students soon began receiving written, formal replies as well as telephone messages. School secretaries asked telephone callers to follow up with a written letter to the child. For most of the children, these were the first letters they had ever received in their lives. Many students, parents, and guardians were amazed that community members and national leaders such as Geraldine Ferraro, Lee Iaccoca, and then-President George Bush wrote personal letters of response to the students. We kept a file of invitations and replies and made a photocopy of each reply. These photocopies were often used as supporting documentation in requests for funding.

Students' reading skills improved with the receipt of these written replies. Mail call became an important part of the school day. Students opened their letters and tried to read every word. Most adults don't write at a first-, second-, or third-grade level, and we're glad they don't! Students used their decoding strategies to figure out "big words" and "hard words." Teachers allowed students time to read without adult assistance. Peer tutoring and cooperative learning developed as the children asked their friends for help.

Students then took turns reading their letters to the class. It was at this point that the teachers would help decode a word. However, we were always amazed that students were able to read the vast majority of words in their letters. Teachers also reported that the students reread their letters several times each day, thus reinforcing their reading skills.

Additionally, students were surprised to find that adults make spelling, grammar, and punctuation errors. For example, a letter from a city official contained the misspelling "yorself." A school board member neglected to put a comma after "Dear Kelli." For each error a student discovered, he or she would receive an additional Hershey's kiss. Not only did students read their letters, they pored over them! One teacher laughingly recounted how disappointed a student was when he told her that everyone who had written to him spelled everything right and "made all the right marks."

Responses to Student Invitations

Some letters were lessons in themselves. Judge Robert Borsos wrote that he would be in Santa Fe, New Mexico, on the day of the show. In his letter, he told the students to find Santa Fe on the map. He then asked questions such as: "When you look at the map, can you guess what big cities we will be driving through or near? How far do you think we will be able to drive each day? How many days do you think it will take to make the trip?" Second-grade teacher JoAnn Yochim steered her excited class into a full-blown geography and math lesson, thanks to the judge.

The students' curiosity concerning their guests prompted many lessons about business, law, government, social services, and other areas. One student, seven-year-old Alice Sanchez, told a teacher in a cozy, confidential chat: "I just got a letter from Marilyn Quayle. You know, she's Dan Quayle's wife and he's the vice president of the United States. And she can't come because she has something else to do at 1:30 but she sent me a picture and I'm going to send her mine." Alice and other students took a personal interest in local,

state, and national news because of these contacts.

Students gained the ability to confidently meet new people, and learned how to display good man-

ners. Many lessons were taught regarding hand-shaking (firm grip, look directly into the other person's eyes, smile), proper introductions (this is my

Hands-on activities are a tremendous resource for bringing a multicultural perspective to elementary students. It enables children to grow out of their ethnocentric picture of the world. Here are six tips teachers can follow to increase multiculturalism in the classroom:

1. Be aware that multiculturalism "must begin" with the adults. Adults must be able to examine their own culture from an outsider's perspective. Modeling these attitudes builds children's self-esteem, gives children a sense of their heritage, and promotes inter cultural understanding.

2. Know your students and their cultural backgrounds. Bring themes from each student's racial and ethnic background into the classroom.

3. Expect conflict and model conflict resolution. Engage students in collaborative activities to encourage cooperation and team building.

4. Bring the outside world into the classroom and help parents see the value of hands-on activities. Parents might be asked to bring a toy and/or photograph that are artifacts from their own childhood. Ask parents to describe some of their favorite themes or activities.

5. Present modern concepts of families and occupations. Recognize that children come from a variety of family structures and backgrounds.

6. Use literature to enrich your students' understanding of cultural pluralism. Literature can: communicate human emotions, model pro-social behavior, give children pride in their ethnic heritage, reveal to children how it feels to be different, and immerse children in other culture's folklore.

teacher, Miss Pachay; these are my friends, Pat and Billy), and the responsibilities of the host (show the guest around the classroom, explain what students do here every day, introduce teacher and friends). Students spent much time rehearsing these life skills. Principal Gary Cramer and paraprofessional Maria Garcia became the generic man and woman guests for the students during many practice sessions.

The students' curiosity concerning their guests prompted many lessons about business, law, government, social services, and other areas.

Students also practiced on each other. Such practices were often spontaneous—in the hall, on the playground, at the lunch table—and playful. While the invited guests were charmed by the courtesy shown to them on the day of the show, the comments from parents and guardians were the most interesting. Upon observing the courtliness of their sons and daughters, most adults expressed surprise, pride, and praise for the teachers.

Community members were pleased to be the "special guests" of individual students. In the weeks following the shows, students often received follow-up letters of congratulations. The mayor of Kalamazoo wrote to Ricky Rodriguez:

I was proud to be your special guest, Ricky. You did a good job on stage. And I was filled with pride when you led us all in the Pledge of Allegiance. Keep up the good work and live your whole life by the values you and your friends demonstrated in the Brotherhood Show. Please contact me if I ever can help you in any way.

This quasi-mentoring relationship was often used to "tip the scale" to the student's benefit. For example, because many people were concerned that a particular student was beginning to conflict with juvenile authorities, that student was asked to invite the local senior agent of the FBI to the show. Although the agent was unable to attend, he did write to the student (on impressive FBI stationery), saying:

Mrs. Ward has told me what a nice young man you are, Franky. I'm glad you are participating in a program of this nature. Although I am unable to attend, I invite you to visit me at the Federal Bureau of Investigation office in the Federal Building downtown. Perhaps you'll become interested in a career with us. We need good smart people like yourself.

Students learned to recognize the power of positive communication. They found that a well-written letter with a purpose generates action: a reply, the arrival of a guest, etc. As their guests wrote to the children, advice was often included: "Keep up the good work....Remember that you can make the world better by learning as much as you can and by being helpful to others....Someday, I hope that we will read about how you have become an engineer, a teacher, or a doctor....The lessons which all of you are learning are extremely important to the future of mankind. Please continue to remind people of that as you grow up."

Students also learned that a thank-you note is mandatory when one has received a gift. Careful records were kept by each teacher listing the gifts the students received (corsages, bouquets, toys, sweatshirts, candy, cookies, stickers, pins, etc.), and students wrote thank-you notes during the week following the show.

The ability to speak in front of a large audience and the ability to speak well into a microphone give students an advantage that will last throughout their lives. Students were taught to speak slowly and distinctly, projecting their voices into the microphone while looking at the audience. During the first rehearsals, most children rushed through their speeches and stared at the microphone. With practice and guidance, they became confident orators.

Students had to memorize pages and pages of material for the shows (songs, scripts, etc.), and thus they gained confidence in their ability to memorize and master a great deal of new information. Most teachers gave the students special "brotherhood folders" in which to keep everything. During the weeks following the show, the teachers discussed these folders with the students, stressing that they had learned so very much—often in languages that were new to them. We found that they had also learned other acts, speaking parts, and routines—as if by osmosis. Teachers told the students that this proved that they could learn anything—all they had to do was practice. This skill was then related to the memorization of math facts, spelling words, and other classroom material.

All Good Things...

The Brotherhood Shows ended as a result of many changes. Because of redistricting, the majority of the international children began attending a different school. We (Donohue and Rybarczyk) transferred to different positions in the school district and are no longer based at Arcadia. Plans were made to house the bilingual classrooms in a K-6 building. But the goal had been accomplished. Ignorance had been dealt a setback. Arcadia was even dubbed "the Brotherhood School" by the local news media. The school won much recognition and many honors. In his letter to Principal Gary L. Cramer, President Bush stated, "It looks like you have created a wonderful school, a dedicated and generous feeling among your faculty and staff and a set of proud traditions. Fine work."

Although the annual Brotherhood Show has come to a formal end, schools in the area continue to incorporate the themes of brotherhood and international understanding into school curriculum and programs. It is thrilling to see the love and pride that result from these experiences. It is also thrilling to look at photos and videotapes of those early Brotherhood Shows. Yet, the best part for us is seeing "old" students and having them tell us that they still remember a certain poem in Japanese, or have taught younger children "El Jarabe Tapatio," or tried out for high school forensics as a result of "starring" in a Brotherhood Show long ago.

Thanks in large part to the Brotherhood Shows, the interaction of many groups of people working toward common goals was accomplished through the school system. The ongoing benefits will be personal, social, and economic, as well as academic. We're proud to have been part of this process.◆

Students learned to recognize the power of positive communication. They found that a well-written letter with a purpose generates action: a reply, the arrival of a guest, etc.

How to Develop a Brotherhood Program

1 Develop a plan.

2 Communicate often. Put everything in writing and keep a master copy of everything. Follow up conversations with brief notes restating the conversation in a positive way. This is especially important with people outside the school (e.g., Dear Mrs. Albkower, Thank you for agreeing to teach a song in Arabic. I'm looking forward to seeing you this Tuesday, October 17, in the Arcadia School gym at 2 p.m...). People with limited English proficiency appreciate something written. They can ask someone to translate it, if necessary.

3 Do things right away.
Don't procrastinate.

4 Make a time line of key events and identify the person(s) responsible for each event.

5 Enjoy the show no matter what happens. We always had a "cast party without the cast" to congratulate all the adults on having, working with, or knowing such outstanding children!

Multicultural Excercise For Kids

Below is a sample of a classroom activity that integrates reading and writing with a multicultural perspective.

Folklore:

Beliefs, Values, and Customs

Objective:

Children learn to appreciate folklore of different ethnic and cultural groups and
to increase their level of awareness of the types of folklore that exist.

Activities:

❶ Introduce the lesson by recalling the titles of folklore that children are familiar with and by identifying the ethnic/cultural groups that the stories are from.

❷ Have children listen to the recording of a traditional folktale. Follow the first listening session with a discussion of the story, including the characters, plot, and ending.

❸ Discuss what it takes for a storyteller to make a story interesting. Replay the recording. Ask children to listen very carefully for the techniques the storyteller used to make the listening enjoyable.

❹ Make a list on chart paper of the various ways the storyteller uses the voice to tell the story (i.e. pitch, volume, and pace).

❺ Have the class select one or two favorite folktales, myths, or legends. Review the stories and, with the aid of a tape recorder, record one or two stories, involving several children in the retelling.

Insights: ____

____

____

____

____

Actions for Our School (District) to Consider: _______________

____

____

____

____

____

____

HANDS-ON MULTIMEDIA

High School students gain more than computer skills in this community work project. They learn tough lessons in planning, responsibility, and teamwork.

5 Americans of the 1990s are using electronic multimedia to transform their personal lives and the world of work. So why not use multimedia as a catalyst for change in students' curriculum, as well?

Edgewater High School in Orlando, Florida, is the second smallest high school in a district of 120 schools. Several years ago, our high school was beginning to suffer from "brain drain." Our top students were leaving Edgewater to attend the only other magnet program in the school district at the time. If we wanted to remain a competitive force in the community, we had to come up with a program so good that the kids would want to stay. The answer to our problem came three years ago, when we began a magnet-school-within-a-school program for engineering, science, and technology. We decided to offer students real-world experiences and project involvement in addition to—and often in place of—traditional classroom methods. We hoped a multimedia program involving real-world experience would stop some of the "brain drain."

GENE BIAS
High School Multimedia Studies Teacher
CHRIS CAREY
High School Multimedia Studies Teacher

Edgewater High School
Orlando, Florida

Real World versus 'Time in Seat'

Because we believe that working on projects connected to the community in some way has more intrinsic educational value than "time in seat," we invite numerous community groups to do real-world multimedia projects with our students. Students design logos, animation, and graphics for businesses, elementary schools, and district office presentations.

Once a group or organization agrees to work with our students on a project, we bring all of our multimedia programs into the development of that project. Students meet with business and organization leaders to discuss the goals and objectives of the project. Then, the students plan a project design and draft a storyboard of ideas.

Students responsible for audio, video, anima-

Hands-on activities help students explore and discover what they are good at, and what they enjoy doing.

tion, and research then begin their various tasks. A project coordinator becomes responsible for bringing all parts of the project together.

As the project takes shape, the students do a constant quality-control check to ensure that their work meets or exceeds the requirements of the organization for which the project is being developed. Students find themselves responsible for every aspect of the project. They often work in amazement as they discover their capabilities are often equal to those of adults.

Over the past several years, we have watched how students change when they become involved with hands-on projects. They take ownership of their work. They develop a better understanding of the relationship between what we are trying to teach them and how those subjects actually are useful to them. Perhaps most important, the students see what they are doing is important to someone besides the classroom teacher. These observations have led us to conclude that working on real-world projects connected to the community, in some way is of greater intrinsic value to students than "time in seat."

Once the program began, we no longer had to worry about "brain drain." In fact, we started attracting students from throughout the district as word of our program spread. In part because of these successes, there are now eight magnet programs distributed among the thirteen high schools in the district.

Giving Each Student 'A Place To Be Successful'

Hands-on multimedia production can become a tool for breaking down social and academic barriers. It gives each student a place to be successful. Let's face it, all kids are not good at the same things. Some are good writers, artists, idea people, organizers, and communicators. Others are good at animation, research, direction, videography or photography. This type of collaboration helps students gain respect for each other's strengths and provide opportunities to students with limited English and academic proficiency to be part of the team. Everybody is good, at something, and hands-on activities help students explore and discover what they are good at, and what they enjoy doing.

We have discovered that students take the educational process much more seriously than they did in a more traditional setting. They feel a sense of ownership for their projects, and like the idea of having control over its final outcome. They also take great pride in doing a job that displays their capabilities to the adult world.

Multimedia in Action

Last year, our students worked closely with the Florida Audubon Society and the school district's elementary science coordinator to produce an interactive CD on "The Birds of Prey" of Florida.

This year, students are working with the Education Department of the Orlando Museum of Art to create an interactive CD about the Pre-Columbian art collection housed at the museum. At the start of this project, students met with the museum's educational director to get some ideas for their plan. They "storyboarded" these ideas so that they could get a visual image of how to present information most effectively in the project. The educational director of the museum met with the students several times during the planning process to offer guidance and suggestions. Once the museum approved the storyboard,

actual production began.

One student collected slides of artifacts and scanned the images into the computer. While another met with museum curators to gather appropriate text to accompany the images. Another student shot film of the artifacts so that digital movies of them could be included. One student created the "shell," an element that would enable all the other components to be added easily to the project.

Once all these steps were completed, each component was assembled into a finished whole—an interactive multimedia product that the museum will evaluate for inclusion in its art display.

Outcomes

During each step in the process, museum personnel met with the students at two-week intervals to monitor progress. The students learned that this kind of research is much more difficult than they thought. For example, they discovered that no one had thoughtfully buried a slip of paper with the artifacts, including all the necessary information. They really had to search to find enough usable facts! They also discovered that once a commitment is made, you have a responsibility to complete a project. Perhaps the toughest part was realizing that they had to create the project the way someone else wanted it, even though this did not always allow them to display their creativity as they might have wanted to.

Many teachers thought we were entirely on the wrong track or were just plain crazy. They were sure the district office and the state would soon have us on their collective carpets for not meeting state mandates.

Among other outcomes, the students were forced to learn much more about the computer software programs and hardware they used. They realized what they knew at the beginning was perhaps only enough to get them off to a good start. Many of the required tasks entailed further study of the equipment. Our students also realized the importance of planning. This is always one of the most difficult parts for students because they want to plunge right into working with the computers and other equipment without really thinking through what they are going to do.

The students' mastery of software, hardware, and the planning process increased exponentially as they worked on the various parts of the project. By the end, they all agreed that they would now feel comfortable working on another project that requires extensive planning and knowledge.

Our multimedia projects teach students many important things besides how to manipulate complex machinery. They learn how to be responsible, solve tough problems, and work as a team. Not all our students can afford to go—or want to go—to college. Some need to go to work right after high school. We help them develop the skills they'll need for entry-level work in multimedia.

More Examples From the 'Real World'

Following are some additional examples of the types of real-world multimedia projects students have been working on at Edgewater High School:

- A group of ninth graders worked with the Florida Society of Engineers to correct a flooding problem in our bus-loading area.
- Ninth and tenth graders designed the electrical and air conditioning systems for a bus they planned to turn into a traveling science laboratory.
- A group of ninth through twelfth graders worked with the Naval Training Systems Center to develop an animated demonstration for an interactive simulation system that the U.S. Navy is

using for training purposes.

• Eleventh grade students began a Water Sentry program. They are working with the Orlando Storm Water Utilities Commission, testing the water of ten lakes in our area on a monthly basis. Students report their findings to both the city and the state environmental departments. We knew the students had become committed to the project when we found out they called the police one weekend because someone was doing something to "their" lake that was not ecologically sound!

• Ninth graders are developing a series of three ten-minute videos for the Orange County Historical Society. They are also creating an interactive computer program outlining the history of the Orange County Fire Department.

• Another group of sophomores is writing grants and applying for awards for the Water Sentry Program.

• A video production was done for a local pharmaceutical company that provided each of the student participants a $100 scholarship upon graduation.

• Students are creating flying logos and animations for local companies, elementary schools, and district office productions.

• A senior designed plans for the new stadium locker rooms under the supervision of an architectural firm working with the school's foundation.

• Several students designed a computer animation production for the 1993 Apple Computer Grantee Showcase at the National Education Computer Conference. Representatives requested another animation for the 1994 showcase.

• A spin-off from the above project includes a multimedia presentation developed by two students, for the Florida Association for Media in Education. This will be presented at the Florida Educational Technology Conference.

• Students are designing interactive multimedia resources that may be used by other students, classes, or teachers as supplemental materials for science and social studies classes.

• Bat Conservation International has given permission for a student to use a large selection of

BCI's slides for a student-produced program on bats. The program will be used in the elementary and middle school grades.

• Another group of students, interested in media literacy, is working with the school district and Time Warner Interactive to create a CD-ROM to help people become more critical media viewers and users.

Exploring Potential, Not Gauging 'Ability Level'

If students show an interest in a particular multimedia project or area of concentration, they are encouraged to pursue that interest, regardless of

We have watched how students change when they become involved with hands-on projects. They develop a better understanding of the relationship between what we are trying to teach them and how those subjects actually are useful to them.

their academic abilities. We are more interested in having the students explore their potential than in knowing what their "ability level" may be. In fact, many of the students we are working with are not even enrolled in any of our classes, yet they are pursuing projects before school, during lunch, and after school.

While we have concentrated on community projects through multimedia, it would be entirely possible for other schools to become more involved with this type of hands-on project with little or no technology. This concept is not about technology, but about getting students involved with real-world applications. We want students to see and understand that writing and communication are not just for the English classroom, that science takes place in the lakes and streams and parks in their neighborhood, and that history is meeting and talking with World War I veterans who can share their knowledge far better than any text might. So, teachers looking for ways to generate more active involvement by their students may want to start looking through the community to find partnerships with willing agencies.

The multimedia projects' real impact on our school, though, is in the way we have changed our teaching methods, our classrooms, and our curriculum to meet what we feel are the needs of our students. These young people are learning to work together. They are collaborating to solve problems. They are learning to locate resources, no matter where those resources are. They are learning to listen, think, and communicate intelligently with both peers and adults. They are learning that reading and writing and math and science are not separate subjects, but are interwoven into a marvelous web that can catch and hold their attention long after class is over.

What We Teachers Have Learned

And what have we, the teachers, learned? Well, we realize that we don't ave all the answers! But that's OK, because we also realize that we want our students to learn how to find the answers themselves. We have learned that many of our students know far more about computers and multimedia than we do, so they get a chance to teach us something. By doing so, they reinforce their own understanding of what they've accomplished.

Multimedia is very time consuming. Our projects require us to spend much more time at school—because our students are always in the classrooms working and we can't get rid of them.

Many teachers thought we were entirely on the wrong track with our efforts, or just plain crazy. They were sure the district office and the state would have us on their collective carpets for not meeting state mandates.

Some administrators have had a difficult time adjusting to the changes this type of curriculum has brought about. What we are doing doesn't seem to fit into their concept of what school should be like.

But others are encouraging. They seem to realize what will have to be done to prepare our students to compete successfully in a global marketplace.

And that's what we have to do—prepare our students to compete with an ever-growing worldwide work force that is becoming more and more informed and capable. To give our students the skills they need, the education delivery system has to change.

We realize that multimedia may not be a venue of change for everyone. But if you think that it might work for you and your students, get out into your community and start looking for projects. They're everywhere!◆

Collaboration helps the students gain respect for each other's strengths, and provides opportunities for students with limited English and academic skills to be part of the team.

The Benefits of a "Real World" Multimedia Program

- Students learn about computer hardware and software programs.

- Students develop a sense of ownership and pride in their work.

- Students learn to work together and collaborate on projects.

- Students get a real work-out of their problem-solving skills.

- Students learn how to research and be resourceful in completing their projects.

- Students gain a "real life" understanding of the importance of planning and organizing their work.

- Students learn to listen, think, and communicate intelligently with peers and adults.

- Students learn that reading, writing, math, and science are not just subjects in school, but are the foundation of many "real world" activities.

Grading and Assessment for Multimedia Productions Class

The final semester grade will be determined in the following manner:
Class participation - 100 points
Demonstration of competencies through presentations and examples - 200 points
Project- 200 points

Total Points	450-500	400-449	350-399	0-349
Grade	A	B	C	D

Rubric Assessment:

450-500 Points (A) — **Exceptional Achievement:** Presentations include substantial amounts of specific, concrete information which is focused and organized impressively; relies on a variety of strategies for presenting information; effectively incorporates all aspects of multimedia including audio, video, still pictures and/or graphics; provides a context for the subject; demonstrates a mastery of understanding of authoring and delivery systems; concludes in a satisfying way; reveals enthusiasm for the subject and authority in constructing and presenting it.

400-449 Points (B) — **Adequate Achievement:** Presentations include information, but usually more general than specific and not as well organized as the exceptional work; relies on a limited variety of strategies for presenting information; incorporates all aspects of multimedia including audio, video, still pictures and/or graphics, but not as effectively as the exceptional model; provides a context for the subject; demonstrates an understanding of authoring and delivery systems; conclusion usually effective but may end clumsily; reveals interest in the subject but reflects less authority than the exceptional work.

350-399 Points (C) — **Limited Achievement:** Student presents information that is brief and shakily organized, indicating that he or she has a very limited understanding of the topic or of reporting information about the topic; relies on few strategies for presenting information; incorporates only limited aspects of multimedia which may or may not include audio, video, still pictures and/or graphics; provides a very limited context for the subject; demonstrates, somewhat, an understanding of authoring and delivery systems; conclusion may end clumsily; reveals interest in the subject but reflects less authority than the adequate work.

0-349 Points (D) — **Minimal Achievement:** Student presents information that is badly organized or incoherent. Although the product is on topic, it reveals little evidence that the student understands the topic or how to create and report information about the topic.

Learning Objectives for Multimedia Class

**Students will meet the following objectives to demonstrate understanding and competency
of multimedia applications:**

Plan a multimedia presentation including:
___brainstorm with others for ideas
___create a storyboard which indicates the "flow of information"
    in the presentation

Use a multimedia software program to prepare a presentation which includes:
___text
___graphics
___sound
___digitized video (QuickTime)
___demonstrates good graphic design and page layout

Use the laser disc player:
___as a stand-alone application
___as part of a multimedia presentation
    (if supported by the application)

___Create digital video using the video camera and "capture" software on the
    computer
___Use the "ZapShot" or other still camera to photograph yourself and import
    the photo into a multimedia presentation
___Use original QuickTime movies in a presentation
    (if supported by the application)
___Create and use original sound files in a presentation

___Demonstrate ability to use a variety of multimedia software programs
    (at least two different ones)
___Identify at least ten resources from the lab which could be used as
    resources in a multimedia presentation you might create

Additionally, students will:

___Accept responsibility for setting personal educational goals and
    expectations for outcomes of the course by achieving standards
    through the completion of specific tasks
___Build their own knowledge base
___Produce knowledge to demonstrate specific higher order thinking, cognitive
    operations or problem solving skills
___Create specific achievement-related products that contain certain
    multimedia attributes
___Use disciplined inquiry to construct meaning
___Establish and achieve works of quality in all assignments
___Use brainstorming techniques to help organize work, look for possible
    solutions to questions, and to solve problems.
___Demonstrate and use communication skills
___Use listening skills to help gain information
___Demonstrate understanding and respect of others' ideas and opinions
___Develop a camaraderie with fellow students by giving feedback and
    encouragement to others concerning their work.

Insights: ____

____

____

____

____

Actions for Our School (District) to Consider: ______________

____

____

____

____

____

____

____

BOX IT OR BAG IT

This primary grade teacher uses authentic materials to teach students math concepts.

6 When I began teaching in the early 1970s, kindergarten was considered a time when children became acclimated to a school routine and to being away from home. Any academics the children gained during the year were considered a plus. The "pressure" to learn was put off until first grade. Over the years this began to change, and I found myself being asked to use various reading and math workbooks and programs in my kindergarten classes.

I did these programs as I was directed. Since we have always had half-day kindergarten classes, those workbook pages took a tremendous amount of the few precious hours I had with the children. The workbooks also went against all that I had been taught and experienced about how young children learn. Sitting in a chair at a table using a pencil to put marks on a page was not my idea of the best way to teach reading and math readiness skills.

Soon the whole language literature-based method of reading instruction began to gain credibility in our area. I was the first in Hopkins County to commit totally to this method and give

JEANIE BARNETT

Kindergarten Teacher

Jesse Stuart Elementary School
Madisonville, Kentucky

up the reading workbooks. I was ready to trust my experience and all that I had been taught about how children learn to read—that is, through hands-on activities and through understanding the joy to be found in books. The children learned that stories are delightful and so much fun with all the parts put together. They learned that words are neat to look at and use, words are made up of letters, and letters have sounds that fit together to make up those wonderful words.

I was finally given the

freedom and time to show the children the whole part of reading first—the fun part of reading, the "reason" for reading. Then desire to learn about the parts would come almost naturally at the time that was right for each child.

It worked! At the end of each year I found that I had a few children "really" reading and more who were just on the verge. Yes, I still had some who still could not name all the letters of the alphabet. These same children would not have learned to name all the letters using a workbook either. But they had gained an understanding of the "why" of reading and had experienced the joy that books and stories can give us.

Discovering Box It or Bag It

But I still had math workbooks to do. Our elementary supervisor, Carolyn Ferrell, began to help us search for another way to teach math in kindergarten. We began to hear about a program originated on the West Coast that used hands-on materials to teach math skills. We had trouble finding out about training and if anyone was using it in the classroom anywhere close enough where we might visit.

Soon Ms. Ferrell was told about another program that was being used successfully by two teachers in Shelbyville, Kentucky, outside Louisville. Lanna Arnold, my principal at the time, another teacher, and myself, visited with these two teachers, Libby Pollett and Debby Head. We got a taste of the Box It or Bag It program.

I was hooked! So was Ms. Arnold and the other teacher. To see children involved in math, excited about math, and learning math at a rate that was right for them was more than I had hoped for.

Ms. Ferrell was excited too. She arranged for two of us to attend a one-week training session on Box It or Bag It that summer. It was a wonderful week. I couldn't wait for school to begin.

This wonderful way of teaching math to children in kindergarten through second grade was developed by Donna Burk, Paula Symonds, and Allyn Snider. All three were, and still are, involved with children in the classroom on a daily basis, just as I am. That meant a lot to me and still does. The program was first published in the form of resource guides in 1988. The publisher for Box It or Bag It resource guides is the Math Learning Center in Salem, Oregon.

Calendar as Math Tool

Thanks to Box It or Bag It, I found out how to help my students learn many

We employ a variety of materials such as cookie dough, unifix cubes, beans, Cheerios, and fish crackers.

math concepts through activities involving the calendar. I had always included a bit of calendar time in the day. But now the children were developing an understanding of patterns, graphing, rote counting, number relationships, and—of all things—place value. I still remember how, after several times seeing and talking about how 0 holds the space in the ones place, Thomas asked me why didn't we write 0 in front of 5. I had never had a child even consider such a thing! But then, I had never presented the opportunity to my children in a way that would enable them to consider it.

A part of our calendar time is something called "incredible equations." The children create number sentences that make the day's date. Through the calendar they develop a true understanding of the concept of zero. I often get 0 plus the date or the date minus 0. Some children get very sophisticated and will add two numbers together that make too many and then take away enough to make it right (for example, for the sixth day of the month, 3 + 4 - 1 = 6). By using tiles we figure out if a number is odd or even, a square number, or a triangular number.

Authentic Materials

Box It or Bag It is based on hands-on experiences using a variety of materials. The resource guides address such basics as the materials you need, how to store them, and how to manage them in the classroom. The authors remind us of the validity of allowing the children what is called "discovery time." I don't ask my children to use materials such as unifix cubes in a particular way for an activity unless I've given them the opportunity to make telescopes, long trains, and pretty patterns with them. Even after we are into the year, I still offer some discovery time when a material is to be used that hasn't been used for a while.

Beans, Cheerios, and Crackers

I teach various math concepts using these authentic materials. The concepts are similar to ones that I struggled to teach using workbooks. They include patterns, shapes, the numerals 0 to 10, arithmetic

Hopkins County School System

The Hopkins County School System is one of the larger school districts in Kentucky, rated in the top ten in student enrollment. Our county is large, too. Our buses travel many miles each day to deliver our children to their schools. Hopkins County is considered a mostly rural school system. Our county seat and the largest town in our county is Madisonville, which has a population of about 19,000. The total county population is about 46,000. About 8,000 students are enrolled in Hopkins County's sixteen schools. We currently have three high schools, three middle schools, and ten elementary schools. Our elementary schools encompass preschool through fifth grade and our middle schools grades six through eight.

After many years of indecision concerning consolidation, our district recently launched into a program of new school construction. Two new elementary schools and a new middle school opened in the fall of 1994. Opening these new buildings enabled the district to close five schools. A new high school is now under construction. When it opens, we will have two high schools, four middle schools, and seven elementary schools. We are looking forward to using more of our school district's resources for instruction instead of maintaining older buildings, many of which were built in the early 1900s.

(facts to 10 and facts to 18), introduction to measuring, understanding measuring, money, place value counting, and place value addition and subtraction.

As we go through the year, the children begin to look for and see patterns in everything. One mother told me that she and her daughter were going to plant flower bulbs. She said her daughter wanted to plant them in a pattern and got busy figuring out

the one she wanted. She reported the flower bed was very pretty the next spring. It is so exciting to see my students discover that our number system is one big pattern. And once they truly understand the relationship of the numbers 0 to 10 and see the pattern in the numbers to 100, 25 + 2 isn't any harder than 5 + 2.

Before the children can pattern, they must be able to sort and classify objects. This is done with many different materials. However, one special way is through the use of junk boxes. The children bring a variety of objects from home. These are then sorted and put into boxes. The junk in the boxes is then used to sort, count, compare, and make patterns. Because the children brought the things, their sense of ownership enhances the use of the junk boxes. For instance, one little girl always shows me her mother's earring when she has her junk box out.

Lessons on the concept of place value counting employ a variety of materials such as cookie dough, unifix cubes, beans, Cheerios, and fish crackers. Each child has a place value counting board with one half white for the ones place and a colored half.

Astronauts and Flying Saucers

The story lines vary from making cookies, filling trays and putting them in the oven, to putting astronauts in flying saucers and flying to a space station. All of these are done in bases of 4 or 5. When this approach was first presented to me, I recalled a nightmarish experience I had in college with bases other than 10. I never understood them. I now realize that if my instructor had played Mission Control with me I could have understood it!

In the game of Mission Control, the rules state that any time there are five more astronauts in the waiting room (the white side of the plane value board), five must immediately board a flying saucer on the launch pad (the colored side of the place value board). Anytime there are five flying saucers on the launch pad, they must immediately blast off and fly to the space station. The children love to play this

*I have worked hard at being
a poser of problems and
letting the children be the solvers.*

game and soon can tell that 102 is really one space station, zero flying saucers, and two astronauts. Adults who are shown this game often mistakenly think that it will confuse children. After several weeks of these activities, the children are ready for a few base 10 story lines and really understand that in 137, the 3 represents three groups of ten and not three things.

Potatoes and Popsicle Sticks

Measuring is another concept that traditionally has been given little time and was taught in isolation from the real world. There are some concept lessons in the resource guides. The children are asked to measure using nonstandard units such as unifix cubes, popsicle sticks, tiles, and even nonstandard objects such as potatoes. When asked to measure using these things, they see the reason for using standard units later. My children measure each other with potatoes and are very serious about how many potatoes long they are. I have even been measured in potatoes, too.

Most of the measuring activities, however, are built into what is called "seasonal mathematics" and are not just done in isolation. This part of Box It or Bag It takes a theme and shows how to teach math concepts within that theme. This was what I needed because I was already teaching almost everything else in my classroom this way. After doing the units outlined in the resource guides, I was soon able to add math to any theme I was doing in my class. For instance, in the theme of make believe, the story of *Jack and the Beanstalk* finds my children planting beans and measuring their growth, making story problems with beans, making a giant using the measurements of children in our class and counting "gold" coins to see how much Jack carried away to his mother.

Children as Problem-Solvers

After the children have many group lessons in a concept, they are given the opportunity to practice what they've learned independently by doing hands-on activities. The components all fit together and allow the concepts to be revisited throughout the year. Some of the concepts are presented daily during calendar activities. They are presented in the

seasonal mathematics and in themes being done in my class. They are also taught in whole-group lessons. My students get the opportunity to use the concept in a variety of ways. Therefore, if a child has truly mastered the concept, he or she can practice it without being bored. Students who have not mastered the concept are given many more opportunities to excel at it because the information is presented repeatedly.

As I have used this method these last six years, I have worked hard at being a poser of problems and letting the children be the solvers. It has been really hard for me to keep from jumping in and telling them how to work out the answer. Through the years I am amazed at how they can solve problems given the opportunity, the time, and the mate-

rials to do so. Travis, for instance, has become focused on square and triangular numbers. He has worked them out using tiles. When we are doing the calendar, he is always ready to tell us if the number is or isn't a square or triangular number. He will wait, however, and let the other children figure it out if I ask him to. While Travis is involved in this, other children are focusing on getting the tiles counted out and are totally surprised with how they come out. Each student is involved at his or her own level, and learn from each other. That's what Box It or Bag It math is all about.

Am I sold on this way of teaching? Yes! I was after the first week of training and was even more sold after the first year of using it with my children. I have been fortunate to have had additional weeks of training; each time I've learned more.

Each year of using it in my classroom reinforces my belief that this is truly the way children learn best.

Beyond Grades K-2

Since my training that first summer, almost all the K-2 teachers in our district have been trained using Box It or Bag It. Buying the necessary manipulatives and making the materials were problems when I first implemented the program. I was lucky that at that time, Kentucky's Education Reform Act was giving school districts money to implement teaching strategies much like Box It or Bag It. Finding the time to assemble the teacher-made materials became easier once I realized everything did not have to be done at once. Those materials were made grad-

ually through the years.

One of the problems I found with Box It or Bag It, is Kentucky's multi-age grouping of children. Many teachers in our district are teaching five- and six-year-olds together or seven- and eight-year-olds. Box It or Bag It is designed for grades K-2.

What are the teachers of the kids who are ages seven and eight to do? *Opening Eyes to Mathematics*, a continuation of the same way of teaching, has been written and published by the two teachers I visited in Shelbyville— Libby Pollett and Debby Head—along with Mike Arcidiacono. Some of our district's teachers have been trained to use *Opening Eyes*, but not nearly the same percentage as those trained in Box It or Bag It.

I thought my students

...ould learn and have fun ...oing Box It or Bag It, and ...hey have. At first other ...eachers were unsure of ...ow it would work. They ...ondered if it would be ...orth the work involved ...n teaching this way. I ...an't say that all are sure ...ven now. I do feel, how-...ver, that as a result of the ...aining, most teachers ...se more manipulatives ...nd student-involved ac-...vities.

Most administrators ...ere becoming used to ...tudents being involved ...n learning with move-...ent and a certain amount ...f noise. We have been ...icky that the Kentucky ...ducation Reform Act ...andates this kind of ...arning for children. ...lany thought that teachers ...ould use less paper be-...ause there would be fewer ...ork sheets used. With ...ox It or Bag It, children

are often asked to record their results so lots of paper is still used. Teachers use more paper for math-related work than ever before. We often make graphs, paper quilts, and math-related big books that are a part of our themes. My students make a theme-related quilt at least once a month.

Getting the Word Out to Parents

At an orientation before school I always explain to parents a little about our hands-on math program. I send home a weekly calendar/newsletter that describes activities we will be involved in. I make sure that I list under math, those activities that might not be thought of as math but really are. Remember those incredible equations that go along with the calendar? The children take

turns taking those home. Those really open the parents' eyes to their children's math understanding. As this has been used, the parents are more accepting and no longer expect the daily work sheets or workbook pages. The word has gotten out.

If you're looking for another way of teaching math in your classroom, I hope you will consider Box It or Bag It. The program allows your children to be actively involved in hands-on experiences using a variety of materials. It's work, but it's exciting for you and your students.◆

Junk Box Materials

Students bring a variety of objects from home which are used to count, measure, compare, and make patterns. Some of the items in junk boxes can include:

Measuring Exercise

Name _______________________________

I think my potato weighs tiles.	It really weighs tiles.
My partner is potatoes long.	I am potatoes long.

Reader Reflections

Insights: ____

____

____

____

____

Actions for Our School (District) to Consider: _______________

____

____

____

____

____

*Most administrators were
becoming used to students being involved
in learning with movement
and a certain amount of noise.*

Jeanie Barnett

Selected Resources

Books

Aldridge, J. and Cowles, M. 1992. *Activity-Oriented Classrooms*. Washington, D.C.: National Education Association.

Azwell, T.S., Foyle, H.C., and Lyman, L. 1993. *Cooperative Learning in the Elementary Classroom*. Washington, D.C.: National Education Association.

Burk, D., Snider, A., and Symonds, P. 1988. *Box It or Bag It Mathematics—First—Second*. Salem, Ore.: MLC Publications.

Burk, D., Snider, A., and Symonds, P. 1988. Box *It or Bag It Mathematics—Kindergarten*. Salem, Ore.: MLC Publications.

Burk, D., Snider, A., and Symonds, P. 1992. *Math Excursions K*. Portsmouth, NH: Heinemann.

Burk, D., Snider, A., and Symonds, P. 1992. *Math Excursions 1*. Portsmouth, NH: Heinemann.

Burk, D., Snider, A., and Symonds, P. 1991. *Math Excursions 2*. Portsmouth, NH: Heinemann.

Cangelosi, J.S. 1984. *Cooperation in the Classroom: Students and Teachers Together*. Washington, D.C.: National Education Association.

Feuerstein, R., Fischer, K.W., Knight, C.C., Presseisen, B.Z., and Sternberg, R.J. 1990. *Learning and Thinking Styles: Classroom Interaction*. Washington, D.C.: National Education Association.

Foyle, H.C. and Lyman, L. 1990. *Cooperative Grouping for Interactive Learning*. Washington, D.C.: National Education Association.

Head, D., Pollett, L., and Arcidiacono, M. J. 1991. *Opening Eyes to Mathematics*. Salem, Ore.: MLC Publications.

Heitzmann, W.R. 1987. *Educational Games and Simulations*. Washington, D.C.: National Education Association.

Lawlor, J.C., Neubert, G.A., and Stover, L.T. 1993. *Creating Interactive Environments in the Secondary School*. Washington, D.C.: National Education Association.

Lescher, M.L. 1995. *Portfolios: Assessing Learning in the Primary Grades*. Washington, D.C.: National Education Association.

Moran, J.D., Sawyers, J.K., and Tgano, D.W. 1991. *Creativity in Early Childhood Classrooms*. Washington, D.C.: National Education Association.

Pattillo, J. and Vaughan, E. 1992. *Learning Centers for Child-Centered Classrooms*. Washington, D.C.: National Education Association.

Perkins, D.N., Schwartz, J.L., West, M.M., and Wiske, M.S. 1995. *Software Goes to School: Teaching for Understanding With New Technologies*. New York: Oxford University Press.

Reiff, J.C. 1992. *Learning Styles*. Washington, D.C.: National Education Association.

Rottier, J. and Ogan, B.J. 1991. *Cooperative Learning in Middle-Level Schools*. Washington, D.C.: National Education Association.

Slavin, R.E. 1991. *Student Team Learning: A Practical Guide to Cooperative Learning*. Washington, D.C.: National Education Association.

Walmsley, S.A. 1994. *Children Exploring Their World: Theme Teaching in Elementary School*. New Hampshire: Heinemann.

Student Portfolios. NEA Teacher-to-Teacher Books. 1993. Washington, D.C.: National Education Association.

Articles

Abbott, E., Ellinwood, J., Horton, D., and Kobrin, D. "Learning History By Doing History," *Educational Leadership*. April 1993. vol. 50, No. 7.

Blythe, T. and Perkins, D. "Putting Understanding Up Front," *Educational Leadership*. February 1994. vol. 51, No. 5.

Brandt, R. "On Teaching For Understanding: A Conversation With Howard Gardner," *Educational Leadership*. April 1993. vol. 50, No. 7.

Burke, J. "Tackling Society's Problems in English Class," *Educational Leadership*. April 1993. vol. 50, No. 7.

Cronin, J.F. "Four Misconceptions About Authentic Learning," *Educational Leadership*. April 1993. vol. 50, No. 7.

Gardner, H. and Boix-Mansilla, V. "Teaching For Understanding—Within and Across the Disciplines," *Educational Leadership*. February 1994. vol. 51, No. 5.

Hartl, S. and Rugen, L. "The Lessons of Learning Expeditions," *Educational Leadership*. November 1994. vol. 52, No. 3.

Herdman, P. "When the Wilderness Becomes A Classroom," *Educational Leadership*. November 1994. vol. 52, No. 3.

Newmann, F.M. and Wehlage, G.G. "Five Standards of Authentic Instruction," *Educational Leadership*. April 1993. vol. 50. No. 7.

Perkins, D. "Teaching For Understanding," *American Educator*. Fall 1993. vol. 17, No. 3.

Perrone, V. "How to Engage Students in Learning," *Educational Leadership*. February 1994. vol.51, No. 5.

Schack, G.D. "Involving Students in Authentic Research," *Educational Leadership*. April 1993. vol. 50, No. 7.

Schnitzer, S. "Designing an Authentic Assessment," *Educational Leadership*. April 1993. vol. 50, No. 7.

Sprague, M.M. "From Newspapers to Circuses—The Benefits of Production-Driven Learning," *Educational Leadership*. April 1993. vol. 50, No. 7.

Unger, C. "What Teaching For Understanding Looks Like," *Educational Leadership*. February 1994. vol. 51, No. 5.

Wiske, M.S. "How Teaching For Understanding Changes the Rules in the Classroom," *Educational Leadership*. February 1994. vol. 51, No. 5.

Videos

Active Learning. Teacher TV, Episode #7, Washington, D.C.: National Education Association.

Business and Education. Teacher TV, Episode #6, Washington, D.C.: National Education Association.

Cross Subject Teaching. Teacher TV, Episode #4, Washington, D.C.: National Education Association.

Getting Resources Into the Classroom. Teacher TV, Episode #27, Washington, D.C.: National Education Association.

Higher Order Thinking Skills. Teacher TV, Episode #24, Washington, D.C.: National Education Association.

Learning From the City. Teacher TV, Episode #36, Washington, D.C.: National Education Association.

New Venues for Learning—Authentic Materials. Teacher TV, Episode #17, Washington, D.C.: National Education Association.

Notes:

____

____

____

____

____

____

Personal Resources

Individuals: _______________________   _______________________

_______________________   _______________________

_______________________   _______________________

_______________________   _______________________

_______________________   _______________________

_______________________   _______________________

_______________________   _______________________

Publications: _______________________   _______________________

_______________________   _______________________

_______________________   _______________________

_______________________   _______________________

Organizations:

Glossary

Assessment
Any systematic basis for making inferences about a student's learning progress.

Authentic Assessment
An assessment that engages students in challenges that closely represent what they are likely to face as everyday workers and/or citizens. In other words, the context, purpose, audience, and constraints of an authentic assessment must connect in some way to real situations and problems. It could be in the form of a performance test, a set of observations, a set of open-ended questions, an exhibition, an interview, or a portfolio.

Authentic Learning
Students encounter and master situations that resemble real life. Students use inquiry to construct meaning and solve problems. Engages higher-order thinking skills.

Authentic Materials
Resources found in the community used to teach students a range of academic subjects. Students use authentic materials to analyze, solve problems, and reach conclusions.

Cooperative Learning
Students work in small groups to help one another master academic material. Interaction can range from pairs discussing an anticipatory set of questions for five minutes, to trios working on complex multi-day units.

Exit Outcome
Specific competency a school wants its students to accomplish by the time they graduate.

Genuine Understanding
Students exhibit the ability to apply knowledge and skills successfully in new situations.

Hands-On Learning
Students acquire knowledge by actually doing or performing tasks, rather than just reading textbooks. Usually involves immersion in community projects.

Integrated Thematic Instruction
Combining academic subjects (social studies, science, history, language arts, etc.) to teach a particular theme or lesson plan.

Multiple Intelligences
Learning theory put forth by Howard Gardner that states students can exhibit their intelligence in many different ways.

Performance-Based Assessment
A form of assessment that allows teachers to evaluate student's skill by asking the student to perform tasks that require the skill. The student must perform with knowledge, instead of merely recalling or recognizing other people's knowledge. A subset of authentic assessment.

Performance Standard

Defined levels of performance against which the performance of a student, school, or district is judged. One may choose to judge a student/school/district by local, national, or world standards of performance.

Portfolio

A record of learning that focuses on a student's work and often on his or her reflections on that work. Material may be collected by the student or in collaboration with teacher(s) and/or parent(s).

Scoring Rubric

Guidelines for scoring a response (including the scale and description of the related criteria).

Simulation

Engaging students in an activity or lesson that mimics or models a real-life situation.

Time in seat

The amount of time students spend at their classroom desks.

Notes:

____

____

____

____

____

____

A school should not be preparation for life.
A school should be life.

Elbert Hubbard